TEEN MONEY MINDSET: 8 ESSENTIAL MONEY SKILLS THEY DON'T TEACH YOU IN SCHOOL

RAISE YOUR FINANCIAL IQ, BUILD LASTING WEALTH, AND GET OUT OF YOUR PARENTS HOUSE!

GREG JUNGE

Dedicated to my late father,
whose guidance, education, and support
have been instrumental in shaping my financial literacy.
This book is a tribute to his enduring influence on his children.

FOREWORD BY TIM RHODE

The driver said to me, "Please don't give me a bad rating for my broken shock absorber," as we took off from the South Philly hotel I was staying at, when he picked me up for the high school assembly I was attending that morning in the fall of 2017. I was the leader of a non-profit called 1 Life Fully Lived and we were doing an assembly that day to help young people just getting out in the world to dream, plan and LIVE their best lives.

I asked the driver to please tell me his story. How is it you are driving with a broken shock? He said he was 43 years old and he now works for the City of Philadelphia making $50k to 60k per year, but the pay doesn't come close to paying his rent and monthly expenses. He graduated from local Temple University in 2003 with a degree in some study that had nothing to do with his current employment. It was chemistry, biology or some other irrelevant degree like that. What I DO remember was that he had been paying the interest on his $100,000+ student loan for over 14 years now. The principal had gone up over the 14 years. He was not paying down the principal on the debt, only as much of the interest only payment that he could afford. He was not making ends meet. Hence, the broken shock absorber. I thanked him for the ride and gave him a nice tip and a good rating.

I arrived at the assembly for the high school kids. They were nice inner-city kids and well dressed in their school uniforms. We completed our assembly where we went over what the vision for their life was. How will you fund this vision? I asked a young lady after we finished, "What do you want to be when you grow up?" She answered proudly "I want to be a pediatric doctor." I said, "that is awesome, what will you do about the DEBT"? She replied, **"What is debt?"** She was 17 years old and about to go to college for 8 years!

I put those two stories here to illustrate WHY this book is so needed now more than ever.

Greg Junge has written a timely book that is very much needed today. This is the opposite of what they are taught in schools. They are programmed to be "Just another brick in the wall," reflected brilliantly by Pink Floyd back in my day.

They are no longer taught about the American Dream. How, with hard work, an enterprising young person can do what Greg Junge has done financially. He has crafted a life of abundance and financial freedom. This book can guide young people who want to follow THEIR American dream and make it come true.

This timeless information can work for you in a way that traditional education cannot.

The traditional "Tried and True" methods are no longer working for young people. Wise parents are looking for new ways to help their children who are just entering the "Real World," find their best path. That is why a book like this is SO valuable and worth the time and energy to not only read it, but absorb the contents deeply, like your life depends on it. **BECAUSE IT LITERALLY DOES!**

I myself did not do well with traditional learning. Like Greg, if I didn't learn the 8 principals taught in this book, I would be like most people in their 60's "hanging on in quiet desperation," dead broke and be a slave to a job. Instead, the reason I'm writing this forward and why I am touting this book is, I DID learn these principals. I did create my own American Dream. Greg and I found the tools needed to make a life by design and you can too!

I went from barely graduating high school to retiring financially free at age 40. I then became one of the Co-Founders of a successful mastermind group called Gobundance, of which Greg Junge is a member of. That is where we met and he introduced me to this awesome book Teen Money Mindset.

So, I hope you do dive fully into this book. Highlight the important parts, come back to it as needed. Learn and master the 8 concepts Greg focuses on. You will be setting your path towards financial freedom. It's not easy. It is truly the road less traveled, but it is the road for your American Dream to come true!

The future starts now. Read on...

Greg Junge's, "Teen Money Mindset", is an absolute game-changer! Too often, high school graduates make it through school without real-world financial literacy as a part of their curriculum putting them at a distinct disadvantage about how money works.

This book, however, hits the mark perfectly. It breaks down financial concepts into digestible chunks, offering practical advice and real-life examples that resonate with today's youth.

The exercises in each chapter provide an easy framework for teens and parents to have an open discussion about finances and investing. Thank you, Greg, for creating such an invaluable resource!

DAVID RYAN, CFP®, CHSNC® VICE-PRESIDENT,
JD BOWEN FINANCIAL GROUP

This book should be required reading for any and all children. Schools would be smart to make it part of their curriculum.The simple but effective strategies outlined in this book could be life changing if implemented.

The best part? Anyone can do it. Get the book. Read the book. Implement the practice. Boom, you're in great financial shape.

CHRIS DUFALA, ENTREPRENEUR, HUSBAND
AND FATHER OF THREE BOYS

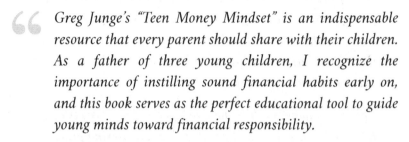

Greg Junge's "Teen Money Mindset" is an indispensable resource that every parent should share with their children. As a father of three young children, I recognize the importance of instilling sound financial habits early on, and this book serves as the perfect educational tool to guide young minds toward financial responsibility.

What sets this book apart is its straightforward approach to breaking down complex financial concepts into understandable, relatable lessons that resonate with the younger generation. The real-life examples and engaging exercises provided in each chapter not only teach important financial lessons but also encourage meaningful discussions between parents and children about money, investing, and saving.

Thanks to Greg, I feel better equipped to prepare my children for a future where they are financially knowledgeable and independent. This book is a game-changer for any family looking to lay a strong financial foundation for their children.

LITAN YAHAV, PROUD FATHER OF THREE

This book would have saved me so much money and time as a young adult trying to navigate the power money has. Greg goes into great details about how money literacy and mindset can help you be financially successful with simple explanations and exercises. Greg explains everything in detail including: how to spend, save, manage your debts, how to create and use a budget, and much more.

Everything you wish they would teach your kids in school but don't, is in this incredible, easy to read roadmap to help teens start their financial journey responsibly and successfully.

Teen Money Mindset will help anyone who is looking for financial literacy help and is a game changer with how easy Greg makes it to understand.

BRENT ANTMAN, ENTREPRENEUR, HUSBAND AND FATHER

As a young person, having the opportunity to download what someone else has spent a lifetime learning can change your trajectory in life. Greg Junge has mastered the game of money, finances and the mindset as well!

Teen Money Mindset contains within it the information you need to consistently make smart financial decisions and pass this on to generations to come.

IGOR AVRATINER, REAL ESTATE ENTREPRENEUR, FATHER OF TWO

Teen Money Mindset is an essential read for individuals of all ages, addressing crucial financial education not typically covered in the public school curriculum. The practices outlined are straightforward and can be implemented by anyone. I highly recommend sharing this book, as its contents are not only inspirational but also educational. Adults, you might learn a thing or two yourself—I know I did!

As an entrepreneur, I appreciate how the book challenges the conventional 9-5 employment model. By applying these principles, the sky is the limit on what you can accomplish. Financial freedom is much closer than you think!

KALE KAUFMAN, ENTREPRENEUR, HUSBAND
AND FATHER

TABLE OF CONTENTS

INTRODUCTION

You may have learned how to solve some complex mathematical problems in school, but do you find opening a bank account complicated? If so, you're not alone.

Schools are great, don't get me wrong, but they only tend to teach you what they believe is important. It seems they aren't really comfortable teaching you all the practical skills and tools you're probably going to use more in your life than algebra. They don't usually teach you how to open a bank account, the difference between a debit card and a credit card, or how bad of a financial crisis most teenagers are facing. These are the things that no one tells you about, but you need to figure out on your own. Harsh, isn't it?

Over the years, I've seen many teenagers who have struggled with the financial challenges that come with growing up. They have no idea how to work with money or invest their money for a better future. Most teenagers love spending money without realizing just how much they are missing out on in terms of growth and wealth.

Sure, that brand-new gaming console looks good, and buying trendy clothes from leading fashion outlets helps you to look fabulous. Even buying yourself some cool new gadget sounds great because all of this will help make you the center of attention. However, take a moment to step back and analyze this behavior.

In the next few months or years, you'll probably say goodbye to most of these people and probably never see them again. Everyone will start to chase their careers, pay their taxes, work out ways to manage debt, repay loans, and lead a life that looks far too complicated and stressful. Is that what you want?

"No!"

Most people don't care about what watch you have, what clothing labels you wear, or what car you drive. At the end of the day, whatever you do, you're doing it for yourself, and if your financial actions aren't benefiting you in the long run, they're not worth taking at all.

To make matters worse, schools never really teach us how to handle and manage our finances properly. Speak about money at home and we're often told never to bring it up or that money is the root of all evil.

I can assure you that money isn't evil. Money is an influential tool that will allow you to accomplish great achievements. It's through money that you can set up a business and offer employment to hundreds, or even thousands of people. It's through money that you can lead a life where you and your loved ones are safe, happy, and secure.

"Sounds like the kind of life I want."

If that is the case, you need to forget what you know about money and what anyone else thinks about your lifestyle choices. All you need is a clear focus, a will to learn, and the right knowledge. Get that combination right and you end up making the finest financial decisions that will lead you to become:

- Confident
- Wealthy
- Financially independent
- Financially secure
- Future-ready

WHAT'S HOLDING YOU BACK

Now, I know everyone wants to learn these things, but most of us never do. Why are we so afraid of change? Have you ever thought about what your life will look like if you start making these changes?

Change is constant, and it will happen whether we like it or not. In most cases, change is a good thing, but since we are used to living a certain way, we are immediately intimidated by the idea of changing things around us. How? Here's a simple example.

Everyone loves the idea of getting rich one day. Everyone wants to make tons of money, invest, and lead a life where they can continue to earn enough to cover all of their needs and desires without lifting a finger. On this part, everyone agrees. However, the moment they are told they will need to work harder, change the way they look at money, cut down expenses, save a lot, repay debts, and let go of credit cards, they start getting scared.

It's odd, isn't it? If you want to be rich so badly, why do some simple changes scare you away from a dream lifestyle? It's all because of the changes. Only those who really want to be rich and lead a great lifestyle dare to embrace change and work with those changes, not against them. That's how they end up achieving success.

Next on the list of things that possibly hold you back is peer pressure. The moment we talk about saving, people laugh. If we talk about cutting down expenses, others will say, "Hey! We only get to live once," and you're immediately compelled to spend all the money you save instantly.

Peer pressure is a real thing. If your friends are buying all the latest phones, coolest gadgets, trendiest clothes, and makeup brands, you're more than likely to do the same. Why?

 You are the average of the five people you spend the most time with.

JIM ROHN

The law of averages states that you're most like, and echo, the behaviors of the five people you spend the most time with. If you spend time with people who love to show off and spend money on luxury, you'll probably do just that.

If that isn't bad enough, if you don't surround yourself with the right people and you tell your friends, "You know what? I'm going to start my own business," they may immediately tell you otherwise.

"No! Don't do that. I know someone who lost a fortune and still couldn't get their business to work."

You pay attention to their words, lose your motivation, and end up finishing your studies just to find a regular 9-to-5 job.

"But I don't know what I'll do without a job. I have to pay for my expenses, college, rent, and so much more. How will I ever manage that?"

I'm not suggesting that I've discovered a way that makes you rich overnight. Chasing your fortunes takes time, but if you trust the process, plan things right, and commit to your goals, you're going to find your fortune, leaving others wondering, "How on earth did they do that?"

It's normal to be afraid of the unknown, particularly the future. However, just because you're afraid of what the future might hold doesn't mean you need to let time run its course. Instead, you need to start planning and making moves now to overcome challenges and take control of your future.

If you're someone who wishes to lead a successful financial life, one that lets you retire on your own terms and offers you ways to make money without any additional effort, keep reading. You can even help a lot of other people along the way. However, one thing you do need to understand is that you'll have to work for it. But it'll be well worth it!

Forget everything you've been told about money, how it's bad, or how it's only meant for the wealthy. Let go of all the limiting beliefs you may have, such as:

- You're not worth it
- You can't be rich
- Wealth is only for the wealthy
- You can never find financial success
- You'll never have enough money

Whatever is limiting you or holding you back, it's time to learn how to break those barriers. My job with this book is simple: To help educate you on everything you need to learn to give yourself the best possible financial future.

You will learn all about money, how it's used, how you can put it to work for you, how to invest, and so much more. You'll also learn some clever strategies and methods that you can start incorporating into your daily life to overcome financial challenges, such as bad debts. I have made sure not to use any complex terminology in this book and to include clear definitions for any new concepts.

This book is filled with examples, exercises, and thought-provoking questions designed to help you clearly understand financial concepts, allowing you to use your newly gained knowledge to improve your finances. You'll learn how to control your finances, grow your bank account, and understand the logic and strategy behind it all. Since you're nearing your adult life, all knowledge, techniques, and tips in this book will help you navigate adulthood more efficiently.

By the end of this book, you'll have gained the confidence to make wise financial decisions, identify and avoid scams, prevent yourself from falling for financial pitfalls and bad debt, and eventually build a solid financial foundation that generates passive income.

Parents, don't let the title of this book fool you into thinking that this book is only meant for teens to read. This book is just as valuable for parents of teens to read because you are their first stop if they have questions about money, finances, and the skills needed to succeed.

Parents and teens should read this book together, have open conversations around money, and complete the exercises at the end of each chapter together.

Parents, you may just learn a few tricks along the way as well!

CHAPTER 1
THE LANGUAGE OF MONEY AND THE CRYPTO CRAZE

> *Money is a tool. Used properly, it makes something beautiful; used wrong, it makes a mess!*

BRADLEY VINSON

You may have never thought of asking this question before, but what exactly is money? Is it just a piece of paper with some symbols, images, and numbers printed on it? Or is it more than that?

When they say, "Money talks," they're not lying. Whatever this "money" is, it knows how to talk. The trouble is, most of us have no idea how to listen to it or how to understand what it's saying, which is where things go wrong.

The good news is that learning this new language isn't hard. All you need to do is learn some new financial concepts and terminology and that's it! Once you get the hang of those, you'll start understanding what money can truly do for you.

With that said, money wasn't always like it is today. Money wasn't always plastic or even paper. In fact, for quite some time in our history, money didn't even exist. To understand how and why it came into existence, let's rewind our clocks and take a trip back into the pages of history.

THE HISTORY AND EVOLUTION OF MONEY

You might be wondering, "Why on earth do I need to learn about history?" Well, history is full of wisdom and lessons for those who know what they are looking for. Since you're here to learn ways to help you grow financially strong and independent, you need to learn the history. The sooner we do that, the easier the financial concepts and terminology will become later on.

Money, as we know it today, is a medium of exchange. Money is used to exchange some kind of currency, such as the US Dollar, with something of equal value. If something costs $100, we pay $100 to get it. It's that easy. Things, however, were very different 5,000 years ago.

The Barter System

In ancient times, the dollar didn't exist. There were no paper notes, coins, or cards. Human beings and civilizations did exist, and they also needed to get access to the things that they couldn't make, grow, or produce themselves but others did. This meant they needed a way to exchange something of value to buy something else. This is where the earliest known system of exchange came into being: The barter system.

The barter system allowed people to exchange something they owned for something they wanted. The trouble was that this wasn't fair. In most cases, this benefited the sellers, and only in some cases the buyers.

For example, if someone wanted a bag of rice, they would go to the nearby market with what they had to trade, let's say, four bags of apples. They would negotiate a price with someone willing to sell a bag of rice. Once a deal was made, they'd end up exchanging apples for rice. In most cases, they'd have to exchange all four bags for a single bag of rice.

You may be thinking, "Wait. That isn't fair."

You're right. In some cases, you may even end up trading an entire cow for a few loaves of bread because that's what was available. Can you imagine just how unfair the trade would've been? Despite this unfairness, the barter system was the only known and accepted way of trading. Even if someone wanted to buy a pair of shoes, they would have to strike a deal with something like a bushel of wheat.

This was until some clever minds realized, "Hang on. This isn't fair."

Coins - A Fairer Trading System

To help buyers and sellers make fair trades, they started introducing a new standard where the medium of exchange was set to animal skins, weapons, and salt.

Since everyone had and needed these items, it became a somewhat fairer way to trade. People still negotiated and some still profited more than they should have, but something bigger was now in motion.

This trading system developed across the entire world and it was well received by buyers. In 640 B.C.E., a facility in the Henan

Province in China started creating metal coins that were used to trade instead (Beattie, 2022). These coins had specific designs and markings, helping buyers and sellers to know the exact value of each coin.

Emergence of Paper Money

This system caught on and soon China went on to become one of the richest empires in the region. This particular coin system took the world by storm and continued until 1260 CE when the Yuan Dynasty shifted from coins to paper money. It was here that Marco Polo, the famous merchant of Venice, wrote about this system and how the Yuan dynasty was using this new form of currency (Beattie, 2022).

Over time, paper money became so popular that every country on earth started producing its own. Eventually, banks also started using paper money as it was getting difficult to carry large amounts of coins around.

With that said, unlike today, people back then could take their paper money, present it to the bank, and they'd exchange that note —based on its face value—for metal of equal value, which was usually gold or silver coins. So, if you held $100, you'd be able to get $100's worth of gold and silver from the bank.

Over time, governments decided they should be the only ones to print and regulate money, not private institutions and banks. This helped start a trade war between countries where each country wanted their currency to have a higher value than all the others.

Buyers and investors saw this currency war and decided to use it as a way to make money. They would buy currencies from leading countries and markets and exchange them for a profit in some other countries. These exchanges started the international currency exchange market which still exists today. This is why you're able to buy any currency on earth for a particular price at any given hour. The values of currencies change every day, meaning that you may make profits or losses depending on whether the value goes up or down.

Up until the 21st century, paper currency was the king of the hill, until, of course, we started using plastic money and mobile payments. Today, most banks and card companies offer mobile payment solutions. This means that you no longer need to carry numerous banknotes to make payments. Just tap the screen and you're done.

The Rise of Decentralized Currency

Governments regulate money. They decide how much to print, what value to set, and when to print more. They decide when your currency note is good and when it isn't. This may seem somewhat unfair, especially considering that there are trillions of dollars on the line. While this wasn't a problem many knew or even cared about, everything changed during the 2007-08 financial crash.

The financial markets of many leading nations came crashing down. As a result, money started losing value faster than one could count. Houses that were once bought for millions were now up for sale for just a quarter of the original price. It was a catastrophe. Why? Because centralized currency institutions and major banks decided to lend out too much money and didn't recover enough in time. To recover from such a loss, central banks—the ones operated by governments—had to print more money. The more money the central bank prints, the more a currency loses its value. Since the gap was so big, the financial disaster was just inevitable.

One mysterious person named Satoshi Nakamoto saw what happened and decided to come up with a new project. A revolutionary new virtual currency that anyone on earth could buy, that no bank or government could regulate, and that had a maximum number of units that, once released, would never be increased. This was clever because if the number of units of this currency was limited and no new units of this currency would ever be produced, the demand would go sky high and so would the prices.

In 2009, Nakamoto finally published a white paper (an official document showcasing the purpose of the project and its scope) for something called Bitcoin (Beattie, 2022). The world was skeptical. This was different, a change that everyone thought was scary and would never work. The idea that no government could control, regulate, or manipulate the value of this currency was questionable. However, some brave few adopted this new idea and what followed was history.

Today, there are more than 23,000 cryptocurrencies in existence, most of them remaining true to the purpose of being decentralized (Daly, 2022). No government or bank controls these and the rates are decided by people like you and me. The more people buy these, the higher the value goes.

Cryptocurrency is now used as a medium of exchange and is accepted by many countries and leading brands. However, some countries have banned the use and mining of cryptocurrencies. With that said, they are legal within the United States and they are a good source for those who wish to make good profits—more on that later.

DECODING FINANCIAL TERMS AND CONCEPTS ESSENTIAL FOR EVERY TEENAGER

Unfortunately, one thing schools don't really teach you is financial literacy. Financial literacy is the knowledge that helps you understand, use, and make money. Not just making money through work and a career, but it's through financial literacy that you use your money to work for you. In simpler terms, your money starts making money without you lifting a finger.

"Cool! I want to learn that."

Well, if you do, it's best to get familiar with some financial jargon and concepts. You can even grab a pen and note these down. They say knowing is half the battle, and that is the case here as well. Once you know these concepts and terminology, you'll better understand what's going on with your money, how investments work, how to set up and manage your bank accounts, and a lot more.

Checking Account

When you walk into a bank to open an account, you have a few options; the most popular ones are a checking account and a savings account. A checking account is where you usually deposit your money, such as paychecks and other sources of income—think birthday or holiday money you may receive from your friends or family members. Your checking account is intended to be an account where you only keep the amount of money you need to spend for your rent, groceries, transportation, and any other basic needs.

The bank may ask you to keep a minimum amount in your account. Therefore, whatever your expenses may be, be sure to have enough money in your account to keep it above the minimum balance. Failure to do so can result in paying a monthly fee to the bank to keep your account open, something you don't want to do.

The checking account comes with a debit card and a checkbook. Both of these are linked to the balance of your account. Therefore, always make sure that you don't try to pay for anything that's over your balance. If you have to pay someone using a check, don't write it out before double-checking your account balance. If you can't make the payment, don't write out the check. This can have a drastic impact on your profile and will cause steep overdraft fees, which is something you want to avoid.

Debit Card

Now I know that you're thinking, "You mean a credit card," but no. Not many teenagers can tell the difference between a debit card and a credit card. These are two completely different things.

A debit card is issued by the bank where your account is. Unlike the credit card, your debit card is limited to the exact amount you have in your balance. So, if you have $100, you can only withdraw a maximum of $100. If you deposit an additional $1,000 in your account, you can withdraw a maximum of $1,100. See how that works?

Let me put it in simpler terms. If I gave you 10 apples, can you give me 11 back? No, you can't. That's because I only gave you 10 apples. I can take back two, three, even nine, and then take back the remainder later when I need to, but I can't ask you to give me more than I deposited. A debit card works the same way. You can only spend or withdraw the money that you own.

Just like the credit card, you can use your debit card to withdraw cash from the automated teller machine (ATM), set a personal identification number (PIN), use it online, swipe it at the store, and even use the NFT touch feature—if available. Every time you use the card, the transaction amount is deducted from your balance instantly. For your protection, I wouldn't recommend using a debit card for everyday purchases. If someone gets hold of your debit card, it is directly linked to all the money in your account. If anyone has your code or scammers get access to it, they can take all your money at once, leaving you with nothing.

Savings Account

While your checking account is intended only for keeping the money you're going to spend, your savings account is where you put any extra money and savings to grow over time.

Unlike the checking account, your savings account comes with a specific interest rate. Based on this rate, the bank will pay you interest against the balance in your savings account. This additional amount is their way of saying "Thank you" for trusting them with your money.

They're not doing it to be nice though. The moment you put your money into a bank, regardless of the account type, they take it out and invest it in other places. They end up earning significantly more than you might imagine. Your balance is only a number reflected in your account. The actual cash is gone. Since they've invested your money, they feel obligated to pay you a very, very small percentage of the profit, based on the total amount you "have" in your account.

Interest

Speaking of interest, it's a price everyone pays for borrowing money, or what someone will pay you if you lend them money—which is also one form of investing. In the case of your savings account, the bank pays you because they borrowed your money. If you use credit cards or loans, you're the one who will pay interest instead. Of course, quite like the barter system, you end up paying more interest and when it comes to receiving some, you get a fraction of what you pay.

I know it sounds bad, but don't worry. You'll learn ways to ensure you can earn significantly more. How? Let me give you a quick introduction.

There are two types of interests: simple interest and compound interest.

Simple interest is paid on the actual amount you deposited or the actual amount you borrowed. The actual amount is called the "principal" amount.

Compound interest, on the other hand, is an interest paid on both your principal amount and any interest that has already been paid. For example, if you deposited $1000 and earned $100 interest (10% a year), the next year you'll earn 10% of $1,100, not $1,000. As a result, you'll end up earning significantly more over an extended period.

Loan

A loan isn't an amount of money you owe—that's actually debt. A loan is more of an agreement between two people, entities, or institutions where one party lends money to the other. The party that receives the money usually pays interest to the lender and must return the principal amount in a stipulated time.

You can use loans to make bigger purchases, such as:

- Vehicles
- Houses
- Land
- Education
- Businesses

The lender decides on the duration of the loan, called the "term," and the person or party who wishes to acquire the loan then has to agree to it. There may also be collateral involved, which are assets you put up as a guarantee, in case you fail to repay the debts. In this case, anything listed as collateral automatically gets transferred to the lender. They can then sell those off to recover their money.

"Ouch!"

That's why you need to understand these terms before you decide to go to a bank and apply for a loan you can't repay with certainty.

Credit Cards

Credit cards can be good or bad, depending on how you use them. They account for $1.079 trillion of the debt that Americans have (Schulz, 2024). Credit cards are essentially loans. Every time you use it, you're borrowing money from a lender. You can use it to buy goods, food, and clothes, and if you spend enough, you can easily reach your credit limit. Using a credit card responsibly will help raise your credit score, which I talk about next. But if you use it irresponsibly, it can lower your credit score and get you into trouble quickly.

A credit limit is the maximum amount of money you can borrow. Whatever you do borrow must be paid back, that too on time. Failure to do so leads to hefty interest rates. While card companies offer "minimum monthly installments" as a payment option, don't let it fool you.

You see, the principal amount that you borrowed remains the same. The monthly minimum payments you end up paying are just the interest on top of the principal amount. This means that if you continue paying the minimum amount for the next ten years, your principal amount will remain the same. To reduce it or eliminate your debt completely, you need to pay the full amount plus the interest.

Credit Score

Everything comes down to your credit score. This is a score assigned to you based on your financial habits. How much you earn, how much and how responsibly you spend, how quickly you pay debts; all of it is taken into account. Based on these factors, you're then assigned a credit score. This number is reflected in your credit report. If you have a lower score, you can improve it by doing the following:

- Pay your bills on time
- Pay off all your debts
- Try to avoid taking out loans
- Pay off any loans quickly
- Minimize your credit limit (keep it under 35% of the maximum credit limit)
- Do not default on any debt

Credit scores range between 300 and 850. Here's a scoring key to help you understand where your credit score may stand:

- 300 - 579: Poor
- 580 - 669: Fair
- 670 - 739: Good
- 740 - 799: Very good
- 800 - 850: Excellent

Ideally, you want to be as close as possible to 800, if not above it. This will ensure that you can apply for any loan later and more easily receive better rates and terms, which will save you money in the long run.

Investment

Any money that you put to work to make more money is called an investment. An investment can make you profits and become an additional form of income. For example, if you buy a rental property, you can start receiving that rent as passive income. Not just that, when the market is healthy, you can sell the property for a higher price, fetching a decent profit in the process.

Any investment comes with risks. Not every investment is successful and not every investment offers immediate returns. Some investments take quite a lot of time before they can bring in any meaningful profits or returns. We will discuss this more later on as investing is one key aspect that can help you achieve financial freedom. Investing is one of my favorite topics to talk about, especially with teens and younger adults, since I'm a full-time investor and love this aspect of finances.

Inflation

At times, countries face economic turmoil which leads them to increase the prices of the goods consumers buy. This financial process is called inflation.

Inflation is measured in percentage. Therefore, 6% annual inflation means that you'll pay 6% more for the same product or service you paid for before inflation hit the country.

There are multiple reasons why inflation comes into play and how it's measured, but since they are not within the scope of this book, we will not be touching upon those.

Taxes

Everybody loathes them. However, they are a vital part of our society. A tax is a percentage you pay to the state or the government for using a service, buying something, or even on what you're earning for your hard work.

"Wait. I do the work and they get the money?"

See what I mean? The fact is that there are many types of taxes that we need to know about. Some of the common ones are income tax, property tax, and sales tax. If you're self-employed, you pay self-employment tax every quarter.

With that said, there is a brighter side to this. Your tax money is pooled into the treasury and that is how the government is able to pay for all the improvements within the country. They use the money to fund projects that help improve the infrastructure, fund pensions, and a lot more. In short, you're ending up funding their projects that help everyone within the nation lead a better life.

"That's nice, but it still feels odd."

Well, don't worry there. There are ways to legally reduce your taxes. We will discuss these later on. For now, let's dive into the world of cryptocurrency, so we can understand how it works.

THE RISE OF CRYPTOCURRENCY

Since we're talking money and finance in general, it's only fair to touch upon cryptocurrency as well.

Cryptocurrency is unlike usual money. Earlier, we learned that this form of currency is "decentralized," which means that it is not controlled or monitored by any central governing body. There is no controlling body that governs its value, its supply, or denomination. This is both good and bad news.

The good news here is that you potentially end up with a form of currency that can skyrocket in value in a short time. It's also completely cryptic, so no one can trace this amount back to you. This protects your privacy and offers you peace of mind that no one can snoop into your account.

The bad news, however, is that cryptocurrency can lose its value just as quickly. Since this is a decentralized form of money, one controls the rise or fall of its value. This means that if you buy a certain cryptocurrency for $10,000 and it immediately loses half of its value in a day, you'll end up losing $5,000. The only options you then have are to keep the currency and hope that it recovers its value over time or to sell it off, but that's another issue.

Not every cryptocurrency can be sold easily. This is due to its liquidity. Liquidity is how easily an asset can be bought and sold. The more liquid an asset, the easier it is to sell it. However, when the market is in a downward trend (called a bear market), liquidity can often run low.

Even with it being decentralized, cryptocurrency still has some similar aspects to more traditional money. First, it can be used to exchange or trade something of value which is pretty self-explanatory. However, did you know that just like the money you keep in your wallet, you need specialized wallets for cryptocurrency?

Whatever exchange or application you use to buy and sell your cryptos, you need some kind of wallet where you can keep it. For this purpose, there are two types of wallets to choose from.

1. Cold or Hard wallet: These are more like USB storage devices that you plug into your computer, transfer the cryptocurrency onto them, and keep it with you. Whenever you need to access your cryptocurrency, you simply plug in the USB, transfer the crypto of your choice to an address and that's that. These cold wallets don't need an active internet connection to work. They are arguably the most secure method of storing cryptocurrency.
2. Hot wallet: These wallets are software-based and are usually provided by service providers. These wallets don't have a physical shape and can only be accessed online. While these wallets are safe, the fact that they are on the internet leaves them open to hacking attempts. The upside, however, is that they are very cheap to get, and sometimes they are free.

Regardless of the method you choose to store your cryptocurrency, you need to ensure it's password protected. You'll also be given backup phrases or keys. Write those down, copy and paste them into a text file, or save them however you want.

Without these keys, you can't open your account if you forget your password. If you lose these, you lose everything within your wallet permanently. Therefore, be sure to save these files in a secure place and back them up.

Common Cryptocurrencies

Many cryptocurrencies exist today. While we won't be going through all of them—it would literally require another book—let me introduce some of the most popular ones out there.

Bitcoin (BTC)

This was the first cryptocurrency on the planet. It's also the most popular and valuable cryptocurrency of them all. When Bitcoin (BTC) goes up in value, virtually the entire market follows the same trend. When it decides to go down, so do the rest.

At its peak, one BTC cost over $69,000 before it crashed down to below $20,000 (CoinGecko, n.d.).

Ethereum (ETH)

Ethereum is the second most popular cryptocurrency in existence. Unlike BTC, Ethereum is based on a unique framework that countless other cryptocurrency projects are allowed to use and develop.

At its peak, one ETH cost $4,878. This was back on November 10th, 2021 (CoinGecko, n.d.).

Litecoin (LTC)

Litecoin is yet another popular cryptocurrency option that people invest in. It has been around for almost nine years and hit an all-time high of $410 in 2021 (CoinGecko, n.d.).

Ripple (XRP)

No list is complete without mentioning another old but active cryptocurrency, Ripple. It has been around for a decade and hit an all-time high of $3.40, a massive 20,800% gain considering it only started with a value of $0.002686 (CoinGecko, n.d.).

Getting Into Cryptocurrency

To buy cryptocurrency, you need to use one of the many cryptocurrency exchanges. The most popular one these days is Binance.

Crypto exchanges are places where you can buy, sell, and even trade cryptocurrencies. These exchanges also offer other ways to make money, such as staking and depositing your cryptocurrency in liquidity pools. While these are slightly advanced topics, for now, know that you can buy any cryptocurrency from these exchanges.

Some exchanges, such as Binance, offer their own digital cryptocurrency wallets for no additional charge. This means that the moment you buy cryptocurrency, it's deposited into your wallet. Alternatively, you can transfer your cryptocurrency to your wallet's address—whether it's cold or hot.

After you've purchased some cryptocurrency, you can also use it to pay for products and services from a variety of stores and brands.

Remember, not all brands and companies accept cryptocurrency as payment. Therefore, be sure to check first before placing your order.

Avoiding Scams

As a cryptocurrency user, you may come across links or posts that claim they can double your crypto overnight. There have been many of these scams that aim to steal your cryptocurrency. Remember, since these transactions are anonymous, you can never recover any cryptocurrency once you've transferred it from your wallet to another. Therefore, always make sure you do your research well.

One such scam claimed that Elon Musk could double your cryptocurrency and to do so, you had to transfer the amount in a wallet first. However, Musk later explained how this was nothing but a scam. Anyone who transferred their cryptocurrency ended up with nothing but losses.

If something sounds too good to be true, just walk away.

Digital Currencies

Just like cryptocurrency, there are also digital currencies. They work pretty much the same, but the only difference is that these are regulated by governments.

Governments create digital currencies to allow investors and others to buy and use them for payments. These are called fiat currencies and include the popular US Dollar, Euro, and others. Unlike traditional money, these don't have any tangible form. These exist in electronic, or digital, form, meaning that you can use and transfer these to others using computers and smartphones as well as cards and some cryptocurrency exchanges.

The entire goal of digital currency is to make transactions faster and cheaper. Traditionally, when money is transferred across borders, it is expensive and requires cash to be transferred, something that itself is a complex process. With digital currency, almost all of these problems are resolved. Not only is the transaction instant, but it's significantly cheaper.

Cryptocurrency, as it turns out, is technically a form of digital currency. While most cryptocurrencies are decentralized and unregulated, some are more stable because they are directly linked to their traditional counterpart form of currency. These are called stablecoins. Tether USD (TUSD) is a prime example of such a currency.

There are downsides of digital currency that exist. Since it's digital, it needs the internet. Where there is the internet, there are hackers. This leaves the entire digital currency realm open to hackers.

It isn't just that either. One core principle of cryptocurrency is to maintain privacy, something digital currency does not do. Since you'll be transferring funds, you will not remain anonymous.

Then, there is the fact that there are high costs associated with the use of digital currency. Since these use blockchain technology, they charge processing fees that are often fairly high.

Finally, digital currency is still a gray area in terms of policy. There is no specific policy that explains whether digital currencies are allowed and considered legal or not. While it's safe to assume that these will remain legal to be used, we may never know for sure. Someday, a government may decide to ink a policy that declares the use of digital currency illegal.

EXERCISE TIME - TEENS

Here is a little quiz to help you jog your memory of what you learned in this chapter. See how many of these you can answer:

1. If you don't understand the difference between _____, you're going to struggle financially.

    A. Insurance and taxes
    B. Buying and renting
    C. Needs and wants
    D. Food and shelter

2. The biggest issue with the credit card is that people:

    A. Forget to use these
    B. Buy things they know they can't afford
    C. Lose them every now and then
    D. Pay to use them

3. For credit card users, it's important that you:

    A. Pay the minimum bill every month
    B. Pay in full every month
    C. Don't pay anything before the due date
    D. Buy whatever you want without worrying

4. Which of these items loses value over time?

    A. Gold
    B. Car
    C. House
    D. All of the above

5. A "good" credit score is:

    A. 391
    B. 673
    C. 752
    D. None of the above

Were you able to answer all of these? If not, there's nothing to worry about. Here are the answers to the questions above:

    1. C
    2. B
    3. B
    4. B
    5. B

Now that you have a fair idea of the basics, let's dive deeper into the book and talk about something called the money mindset. This may sound somewhat odd, but trust me; you need the right mindset to attract money your way.

CHAPTER 2
MONEY MINDSET MAGIC

 Money is a terrible master but an excellent servant.

P. T. BARNUM

Did you know that having a specific type of mindset is required to attract money and financial success? I know it sounds weird. How could a mindset attract money? However, ask any of the most successful people on earth and they will tell you the same.

There is a very good reason why some people tend to just attract money their way while most struggle to find ways to make some. That reason is the difference in their mindset.

The fact is that money is closely linked to our emotional state. Money impacts our mindset and our psychology and vice versa. Since this is the case, let's learn how these are interlinked and how you can build a mindset that helps you attract money.

THE PSYCHOLOGICAL ASPECTS OF MONEY

When you have money, you feel good. When you don't have money, you feel bad. There's no rocket science here to decode. That's just how things are. However, there are those who, despite having money, still feel bad. Their mindset lets them believe they don't have enough. If this sounds familiar, don't worry. You'll learn how to get rid of this mindset.

Two types of financial mindsets exist: A scarcity mindset and an abundance mindset.

The scarcity mindset is a type of mindset where one limits oneself in all ways imaginable. Give this person $100,000 and they'll still think "I don't deserve that," or "That's not enough." These are the kind of people who believe that wealth is only for the rich or that they can never be rich. They doubt themselves, their abilities, and their skills. To them, life is all about living paycheck to paycheck and not taking any risks. They believe it will never pay off, and therefore are stuck in a scarcity mindset.

When you have a scarcity mindset, most things in life are just not enough. You always believe that there's less of everything for you. This impacts how you function, how you think, and how you react to opportunities.

For example, a person who has a scarcity mindset will skip opportunities that can potentially lead to significant fortune and wealth, and tell themselves:

"I can't be rich."

"I'll never be rich."

"I don't think I can do this."

"I don't have what it takes to find success."

"Success is only for the rich, not for people like me."

They'll come up with the worst excuses to pass on the opportunity because deep down, they believe it will never work. However, what they fail to realize is that this is their negative and scarce mindset talking to them.

When you have a scarcity mindset, you never feel fulfilled. As a result, you make the wrong financial decisions and end up piling up debt. If that wasn't bad enough, this mindset also impacts our relationships, work, and life in general.

People who have a scarcity mindset typically experience increased levels of stress and anxiety. You can spot someone who has such a negative mindset easily as they are usually more focused on things they don't have as opposed to counting their blessings. When people want something and they don't believe they deserve it or can acquire it, it's no surprise when things don't go their way.

"See, I told you. I can never be rich."

On the other end of the spectrum, we have those who have found a better way of looking at things. There are people who, even when they don't have much going on in life, are always thankful and tend to count their blessings. These are people who believe they have enough of everything they need, even money. As a result, they feel more fulfilled, energetic, and happy.

It should come as no surprise that when you come across someone with an abundance mindset it feels nice just meeting them. It's not them, it's their positivity that makes you feel this way. Such people have a different aura about them. Everyone wants to talk to them, sit next to them, and be like them. Whenever they walk into the room, you know they're there because the air feels different. Why? Because they have mastered the abundance mindset.

The abundance mindset is one where you know and believe you have enough of everything you need. This includes money, fame, fortune, wealth, opportunities, income, friends, love, respect, and everything you desire in life. However, the magic doesn't stop there.

There's a concept called the law of attraction, which simply states "Like attracts like." The law defines that when you feel negative, all you end up attracting is negativity. When you think you don't have enough, the universe will find a way to take more away from you.

The converse, however, is true as well. When you believe you have enough, the universe finds a way to give you more, even if it's money. Call it a superpower or a secret weapon, but it works. This is exactly what successful people do. This is exactly why they are always smiling and positive. It isn't because they have money, it's because they believe they have enough of everything.

Needless to say, anyone with an abundance mindset goes on to attract love, care, compassion, money, wealth, and much more. The best part is that anyone can acquire this abundant mindset, with a little practice of course.

The Common Psychological Traps

Those who don't have a positive outlook are prone to falling into one of the many psychological traps related to money. You have probably come across quite a few of these in your own life and the lives of the people around you. Someone you know may be going through this right now, or you may have faced some of these traps yourself.

The goal isn't to make anyone feel bad about themselves. In fact, it's to educate you, so that you can spot the signs and make sure to avoid the traps and find a better way to live a more positive and successful life.

I Only Want to Have Enough to Be Comfortable in Life

People from the middle class, those who are neither rich nor poor, prioritize comfort in life. They are led to believe that they can somehow come to a place where they will be comfortable and that they only need X amount of money to do that.

I hate to break it to them, but there's no such thing as a "comfortable" place. If you're someone who is aiming for financial freedom, comfort needs to be your last concern.

The trouble is that when you're seeking this so-called comfortable zone, you work day in and day out, unable to quit your job or take any risk, so you can save just about enough to have a comfortable retirement. The idea is okay, but the end result isn't. Do you want to settle for okay? An okay car, okay health, okay relationships? I certainly don't!

I Need to Make More Money

Everyone needs money. Everyone wants more of it, but how much is more? Nobody knows. When you don't know what you're aiming for, you'll never know if you hit the bullseye or missed it completely.

Clarity is important. This is why it's also important to set realistic financial goals for yourself so that you know what you're aiming at and when you have achieved a particular goal.

Bigger Isn't Better

Some believe that being bigger or richer is not better. They believe that it's far more stressful, which is why they give up the idea of dreaming big. The fact is that bigger is actually better. The bigger your success, the more joyous your life. It's as simple as that.

More Money Invites More Problems

This is not true. The people who don't have money face severely more problems than the ones who do have money. Those who have money can afford food, water, shelter, and medical care, and are in a far better position to handle their essential needs to lead a good life. Those who don't, unfortunately, are struggling to put up enough money to buy their next meal.

It Takes Money to Make Money

There is a belief that you need to have money to make more money. Technically, this is true, but let me explain since this is a gray area.

Today, three-quarters of the world's millionaires are first-generation millionaires (Cardone, 2015). This means that they never had enough money to start with. It proves that they had an idea, they believed in it, dreamed it, and chased it. As a result, they found their fame and fortune while most gave up at the start or in the middle.

The true part, however, is the fact that you can put your money to work. When you invest your money into something it will start making you more money. We'll discuss this more later on.

There's Not Enough Money

People who don't have money believe that money is scarce and that there isn't enough for everybody. To be honest, that can't be further from the truth. As of 2015, the total amount of money on earth stood somewhere near $134 trillion (Cardone, 2015). That's $134 and twelve zeros. If you divide that equally, every single soul on earth ends up getting around $16,750.

The point I'm trying to make is simple: There's enough money for every single person on the earth. What matters isn't the scarcity of money, but the will and the courage it takes for people to get up and do something to get that money.

Money Is the Root of all Evil

Okay, how many times have you heard someone say this? Probably a lot. The fact is that this is yet another quote people with a scarcity mindset come up with. Money can't do anything on its own. You need to assign your money some role for it to do something.

Money is power. The more of it you have, the freer you are to choose your lifestyle. You can pay off debts, improve your lifestyle, take care of your loved ones, and use money to do good in the world by donating, giving to charity, and so much more.

Money Can't Buy Happiness

Yes and No! Having money can make you happy, sure. But life happiness stems from many avenues, and finances is just one of those avenues. Money can buy you freedom! When you have money, you are free to do what you want in life. You can decide if you want to work or not, full-time or part-time, who you want to work with, and for what purpose. Money buys time and freedom, which frees you to create the life you want.

The point I'm trying to make is simple: All of these are just things naysayers have cooked up. If you believe in any of these, you need to change the way you think. You need to adopt a new perspective on life.

BEHAVIORAL FINANCE

Having money, or the lack of it, changes the way you behave. When it comes to making financial decisions, you're likely to make better ones when you have strong financial literacy and an understanding of how money works.

Let me explain this using a simple example; the fictional story of an 18-year-old named Sam.

Sam went to college and led a busy life. He wanted to be rich but had no idea how. Many people told him to gain some financial knowledge and learn more about the financial world, but it felt too boring and dry.

"I'll do that once I grow older."

One day, he decided to buy himself some lottery tickets. He never really believed in these, but the idea of winning a million dollars did feel nice. However, there was a part of him that wondered what would happen if things went his way.

"I could change everything about my life and never have to work again."

A few days later, the winning ticket number was announced and Sam, of all people, ended up with the winning ticket. Overjoyed by his win, he told his family and friends that he was now a millionaire.

Two days later, he went in to collect his check. However, to his surprise, the check was just $800,000.

"There must be a mistake. I won a million."

"Oh, don't worry, it's just the 20% tax involved."

Somewhat confused, he decided it was still more than enough to change his life. In the following week, he bought a luxurious house, repaid his parents' debts, bought two luxury cars, ate at the finest restaurants with his friends, and even booked flights to travel the world.

He called his employer and said he was quitting.

"I'm rich. I don't need to work anymore."

To him, life changed completely. After all, he had so much money. He could do whatever he wanted and never have to worry about anything ever again. Of course, that's until life happened.

Just a month in, he had spent over $750,000 already. The bills started coming in and he realized this wasn't working out at all.

"At this rate, I'd be broke in less than 30 days."

A friend of his suggested he should invest his money instead.

"No! That's all just a big scam. I'll find something to do instead."

Another week passed and he now had less than $10,000 to his name. He had to sell his cars and buy cheaper ones. He also sold his house because he couldn't afford the high maintenance costs and bills.

See what happened here? Even though Sam had a million dollars, he made all the wrong choices. When he had the opportunity to invest, he chose to spend instead. This is because he lacked financial literacy.

The fact is that financial literacy helps you understand your income and expenses and can help you make the most of your situation by investing, saving, and achieving your financial goals. It's through financial literacy that you understand which decisions are good and which aren't.

The Nobel Prize-winning psychologist, Daniel Kahneman, carried out a study and proved that we human beings make 90% of our financial decisions based on emotions and only 10% using logic (CNB, n.d.).

When you end up winning such a large sum of money as Sam did, your emotions are all over the place. Your emotions influence your decision-making and you end up making terrible financial decisions.

Those who master the art of keeping their emotions out of their financial decisions, end up finding financial success. It's hard, but it isn't impossible.

For example, if you were to be given a choice to use $250,000 to buy a Ferrari or invest the same amount of money somewhere, what would you choose? If you follow your emotions, you'd probably go for the Ferrari as it's a status symbol and offers immediate gratification. However, logic dictates that you invest that money now and reap the benefits in the future. Yes, the gratification isn't instant, but it's guaranteed to last significantly longer.

"I get it. You need the right mindset, but how do I do that?"

Learn More About Financial Literacy

Financial literacy is key to your financial success. It's what allows you to learn all about money, understand how to use it wisely, and even how to make more money using what you already have.

How do you learn? There are quite a few ways to improve your financial literacy, including:

- Books
- Blogs
- Courses
- Tutorial videos
- Articles
- Business news
- Online resources such as Investopedia

However, one of the most rewarding ways to learn is to have someone teach you. The trouble is that not everyone knows how.

To start with, you need someone who is an expert in financial literacy. You need to find yourself a mentor or a coach, someone who can help you understand your financial situation and who aligns with your goals and desired outcomes. If, for example, you want to learn how to invest in real estate, don't ask someone who invests in the stock market to be your coach or mentor. Fortunately, there are organizations out there that can help you do just that.

Whichever route you choose, be sure to commit to it and see things through. Learning is a life-long journey that never ends, and shouldn't end. Every year, something new comes up. Those who wish to achieve success need to remain open to new ideas, learn and embrace change instead of running away from it out of fear, and not get distracted by new investment strategies and jump around—also called the shiny object syndrome. Become a master, staying focused and consistent will serve you best.

STRATEGIES FOR DEVELOPING A POSITIVE MONEY MINDSET

Your mindset plays a vital role at the heart of your financial success. It's through a positive money mindset that you can start learning, adapt to changes, embrace failure, and learn from those failures. It's through this mindset that you find the will and confidence to continue learning and improving. As a result, you start making better financial decisions based on logic, not emotions.

Financial education is important, make no mistake, but if you don't have the right mindset, all that knowledge essentially goes to waste. Your financial education helps you understand where the money is coming from and where it's going, how to save money, how and where to invest, and so on. However, it's your mindset that dictates how you'll use that knowledge, if at all.

Developing a positive money mindset isn't hard. It takes some practice, but once you get the hang of things, you can start reaping the benefits sooner than you might imagine.

To help you, here are some great ways to get started.

Forgive All Financial Mistakes

As human beings, we are bound to make some mistakes. This also applies to our finances; we end up spending too much, too little, or unnecessarily on things we want and need.

The very first thing is to let go of that guilt that's eating you up from within. We all make mistakes, but these mistakes help us learn and grow. Instead of going on a guilt trip, start learning from your past mistakes. Analyze your mistakes and how you can make wiser decisions. Write these mistakes down in a journal or notebook, so you'll always have it to reference in the future.

You may have missed a credit card payment or perhaps overlooked the due date on your utility bill. Whatever the case, you're not alone. Making a mistake once is acceptable, we've all done that. Making the same mistake over and over again is unacceptable. This is what separates you from others, learn from your mistakes and make sure never to repeat them.

Shift your focus from guilt and start finding ways to learn from past mistakes. Make room for growth and take a more positive approach. Instead of thinking about what could've been, think about how you can make wiser decisions moving forward. Think about how great the outcome will be if you face the same situation again.

Set Financial Goals

After forgiving yourself, it's time to start setting up some new financial goals. Make sure you understand how to set the right ones.

Just writing down "I want to be rich" isn't exactly a goal. Why? Think about it. If someone were to give you $1, would that make you rich?

"Umm... No!"

Technically, it will because you'll be a dollar richer. However, that isn't exactly what you're aiming for, is it?

Instead, learn how to set SMART goals. These are goals that are:

- Specific
- Measurable
- Attainable
- Relevant
- Time-bound

Let's say you decide to save $10,000. You write down "I will save $10,000." Now, the goal is specific because you know what you're aiming for. It's also measurable because you can measure how much you've saved and how far you still need to go. However, let's add more layers to this and see how it sounds.

"I will save $10,000 to help pay for college, 5 years from now."

Ah! Now the goal sounds like a SMART goal. How? It has all the elements in it: It's specific, measurable, and thanks to the additional details, meaningful to you (relevancy), and you've set a deadline as well.

You're more likely to achieve goals that have a deadline than ones that don't. However, is this goal attainable? Let's find out.

$10,000 / 5 = $2,000 a year

"Hey! That's not bad."

Trust me, it's about to get a lot easier.

$2,000 / 52 (number of weeks in a year) = $38.46

In short, you need to save just $38.46 every single week for the next five years to comfortably achieve your goal. That makes this goal attainable and a lot easier.

Set the Right Budget

To master your money and your money mindset, start by creating a budget for yourself. Creating one may be somewhat intimidating at first, but it'll pay off in the future.

A budget is the greatest way to track your income and expenses. It helps you organize and allocate your money and identify where you may be spending money needlessly, such as an unused subscription or an online gaming site that you don't play on anymore.

Don't worry if you've never made a budget before. Just use the 50/30/20 rule. This rule dictates that you should use 50% of your income for your needs, such as car maintenance and gas—if you have a car—or saving for a car—if that's important to you—rent, utility bills, food, etc. You should use 30% of your income to handle your wants, like eating out with friends, buying a new cell phone, etc. Finally, you should use 20% of your money to save. If you have debts, use your 20% to pay off your debts.

There are many other ways to create a budget, but for now, know that you need a budget to help you be more confident with your money. To help you further, you can track this very easily in a spreadsheet on your computer, download free budgeting apps, or track it with pen and paper in a notebook or journal.

Learn About Money

I mentioned it earlier and I'll say it again: Be a student for life. Continue learning something new about financial literacy, about money, and how to make more of it every day. You can:

- Read books like *Rich Dad, Poor Dad*
- Follow successful people on social media
- Read blogs
- Take up courses
- Attend seminars and trainings

Whatever you can find, go for it. While everyone has their own idea of how to manage finance, most of them share the same principles.

Set Long-Term Goals

Not all goals are meant to be short-term. Set ones that are long-term, that you wish to achieve in 10, 20, or even 30 years from now. Once again, use the SMART goal approach. Write these down, put up pictures on a vision board, and remind yourself every day of what you want to achieve.

Another great trick is to find pictures of what you want and save them on your phone. If you'd like to take a vacation to Italy as a goal, find the most beautiful picture of Italy on the internet and save it on your phone. Better yet, make it a wallpaper. You can also set this as a background on your computer so that you can see it every day and find motivation in ways you can't believe.

As you continue doing this, you'll start to see a more positive version of yourself emerging. Not just that, you'll start making decisions that are refined and more in line with your values and goals. As a result, your decisions will help you grow, save, invest, and much more.

"But what happens to someone who doesn't do any of that?"

Chances are, they might have a very bitter relationship with money and, as a result, they might experience a lot of problems. These include, but are not limited to:

- Impulse shopping: Buying things just because they want to
- Maxing out credit cards and later regretting it
- Having an inability to manage finances properly
- Refusing to talk about money or even seek some kind of financial support for assistance
- Developing an irrational anger towards those who are more financially secure
- Being a miser and afraid to spend money on necessities

Needless to say, people who don't have the right mindset are always surrounded by debt and financial problems. These can directly impact their relationships, job satisfaction, and life in general. We don't want that, do we?

How to Shift Your Mindset

To avoid developing negative financial habits and lead a life that's brimming with joy, success, and happiness instead, here are the steps you can start taking right away to shift your mindset.

Visualize Your Success

Success is subjective: To you, it may have one meaning, while to me, it may mean something else. Visualize your own success, whatever it may be. There's no right or wrong here.

Think about where you are, what you're doing, what you've achieved in this future of yours, and what makes you believe that you've been successful. Note everything down and make it a habit to visualize your success every day for 15 to 20 minutes. This helps you train your subconscious mind to familiarize itself with this vision and then find ways to make it happen. Visualization is a great practice on its own, and I encourage you to research this technique further. It can be very powerful, but just like anything else, you have to practice and believe in it for it to show results.

Learn Now

There's no such thing as a perfect time and place. If you truly wish to find success, start now. Start reading more books, articles, and blogs, talk to successful people, listen to them, and find out what worked for them and what didn't. When you're talking to successful people—which is my go-to way to learn—be curious and ask questions. Trust me, people love answering questions about themselves, and it's by far the best way to learn and build relationships with others.

Eat Out Less

It's very tempting to eat out, but for now, it will have to wait. Since you're a teenager, chances are that you're not making that much money. You want to save as much as possible so that you can use that money to create and maintain an emergency fund, invest, and pay off debts. It's okay to eat out once in a while, but consider how fast your bank account would grow if you limit the number of times you eat out. It adds up pretty quickly.

Checking Your Accounts

Get into the habit of checking your account every day or at least weekly. Find out where you've spent your money and keep an eye out for any additional charges to your account that you can't identify. If you find these, report it to the bank so that you're no longer charged for services or products you don't use, or that you were incorrectly charged for in the first place.

EXERCISE TIME - TEENS & PARENTS

Having the right money mindset is important. To ensure you get started on the right track, use the journal template below. You can copy this and make it more elaborate to better suit your needs. This exercise is for both parents and teens to complete and share with each other.

Current money mindset:

1. What are your current beliefs about money?

2. Where do these come from?

3. How have these beliefs impacted your financial decisions so far in life?

Desired money mindset:

1. Identify and write down the money mindset you want to have.

2. Why is this mindset important to you?

3. Use the internet to find inspirational quotes that resonate with you. Write down the most inspiring ones.

Steps to improve your money mindset:

1. List three practical steps that can help you shift your mindset to the one you want to achieve.

2. For every step, write down why they're important to you and how you intend to implement them in your daily life.

3. Set a timeline for when you'd like to achieve this mindset.

Next, let's take a dive into the world of credit and understand how loans and credits work. Not just that, we will also learn how they can impact your financial future.

CHAPTER 3
CREDIT CRUSH

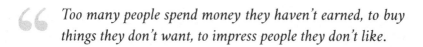 *Too many people spend money they haven't earned, to buy
things they don't want, to impress people they don't like.*

WILL ROGERS

Loans and credit cards sound great. It feels like we can always turn to these when the going gets tough. Well, that's what we've been led to believe.

Yes, they are helpful, but none of that money is yours to begin with. The moment you sign up for a loan, you have to pay it back one way or another. Unless you're using your credit or loan wisely to build wealth in some way, you're signing up for liability and added financial pressure.

In this chapter, you'll learn how credit and loans work and how these directly impact our future. You'll also see if there's anything worth knowing that others don't want to share.

COMPREHENSIVE GUIDE ON CREDIT AND LOANS

Credit is a kind of contractual agreement between two parties, a borrower and a lender. The borrower agrees to receive a sum of money which they will then pay back within a certain timeframe along with interest, and the lender agrees to lend the money for that set amount of time, in return for a higher return.

One meaning of the term "credit" relates to the contractual agreement. Another may refer to a person's creditworthiness or credit history, which indicates whether they are likely to repay their debts on time or not. This allows other financial institutions and lenders to decide whether to lend that person money or deny their application.

In our case, we're interested in learning about both. Fortunately, we've already come across some important terms earlier in the book, such as credit score, credit score ranges, and why they matter.

However, let's dive a little deeper since these are important to understand for your financial future.

Let's say you decide to get a credit card. The moment you get it, you'll also get something called a "credit limit." This credit limit is essentially the maximum amount of money you can borrow using your credit card. The more you use your available credit, the higher your credit utilization becomes. The moment you pay back what you owe, and in full, your entire credit limit is once again available for you to use.

Your credit limit and utilization rate impact your credit score significantly. If you have a low credit utilization rate, ideally less than 10% of the credit available to you, it will reflect positively on your credit score. Utilization rates of anything like 30% or higher will negatively affect your score. How quickly you repay your dues matters here as well. The lender, often the bank, either becomes confident in your ability to repay your credit or the opposite. Based on these alone, you may end up getting rejected for credit or loans if your profile is deemed "risky."

"So, I just need to keep an eye on my credit card usage to get a good credit score?"

Well, yes and no. Credit limits and utilization rates are important and they do influence your score, but they aren't the only elements that do.

Here are the factors that are taken into account to determine your credit scores. The numbers in the brackets show how much each of these components contributes to your credit scores.

- Payment history (35%): This has the biggest impact on your credit score. If you're someone who makes every payment on time, including your utility bills, credit cards, and others, you're going to see a massive improvement in your score. However, one delayed payment (just 30 days late) and your score will fall greatly. Bankruptcy, foreclosure, or an account that's sent for collection can severely impact someone's overall profile and they can take years to fully recover.
- The amount you owe (30%): Your debts, or the total amount you owe to lenders, affect your credit score as well. This is also where your credit limit and utilization come into play. If you have a credit limit of $1,000 and you've only used $100, you'll have a great credit utilization of just 10%. As long as you pay off the $100 credit, you will

be fine. If you make big payments to pay off high-balance debts, it will reflect positively in your next credit report.

- Length of credit history (15%): The length of your credit history shows just how long you've maintained your credit, exercised good financial habits, and repaid debts—if you have any. The longer your history is, the better score you end up getting.

- Credit mix (10%): Your ability to handle, manage, and pay off multiple credit types is also seen as a motivator for the number crunchers. Let's say you're paying off installments for a student loan, car loan, and personal loan, and you're doing this while also handling a revolving account (credit card), it reflects as a positive score on your profile.

- New credit (10%): If you end up getting new credit, you may find your score taking a hit. The fact is that when you take up any new credit, it may hinder your ability to pay off your previous credit easily. This is seen as a bit of a risk. If you apply for numerous credit cards or new loans in a short time, it can also lead to your score falling. Therefore, be very careful how and when you apply for loans.

Your credit score matters more than you think. Based on your score, all lenders, whether banks or other financial institutions, will decide on approving or denying your request. The better your score, the easier the process. However, for those who are just starting out, such as teenagers, things can be tough.

Teenagers are assigned a low score and they then have to stick to good financial practices to ensure their scores increase. This takes time but you eventually get a good credit score if you remain consistent and continue to make timely payments.

As a teenager, you can have your parents or other family members add you as an authorized user to help you build your own credit score. However, once you're an adult, you'll need to put in some extra effort to build your own credit scores. With that said, it's worth it. When you have good credit scores, you end up with the following benefits:

- Access to almost all credits and loans
- Higher credit limits
- Lower interest rates on loans
- Quicker turn-around time for loan applications

These are just some of the many benefits that you can receive.

A good way to get started as a teenager is to check out Teen Credit Builder Loans. These are specialized loans designed to offer you a chance to build your credit history and improve your score. You need to be 16 years old to access these services. However, you may need a parent's account to help you with this.

There are other types of loans you can take advantage of such as teen auto loans and a teen Visa credit card.

The interest rates are generally lower and these usually come with smaller monthly repayments. As long as you continue paying on time, the lending party will report to the credit bureau about your good financial behavior, and that helps you gain higher credit scores.

Types of Loans

The following are the most popular loan types you're likely to come across. You may not need all of them, but it's good to know what you have available.

- Auto loans: These are loans aimed at helping you buy a vehicle. You make a down payment and the rest of the payment is paid by the lender (usually a bank). Your car automatically becomes listed as collateral and can be confiscated if you're unable to make repayments. These loans range anywhere from 36 months to 72 months. Most teens prefer longer loan durations as they have lower monthly repayments. However, since you'll be paying longer, you'll end up paying more overall.
- Student loans: Students often get these loans to help them attend college and graduate schools. You can get these from private lenders as well as the Federal government. People generally prefer applying for Federal student loans as they have a lot of flexibility. These also don't require a credit check whereas the ones from private lenders do.
- Personal loans: These are not used to buy property or cars. Instead, these are used for anything you wish to purchase. People usually use personal loans to handle emergencies and urgent situations, such as weddings or home improvement. These are unsecured loans, which means they don't require any collateral, unlike auto loans.
- Mortgage loans: These are designed to help you buy property. You make the down payment and the bank, or the lender, handles the rest. You can set the term of repayment anywhere from 10 to 30 years. Here, your property is held as collateral and the bank can foreclose on (take possession of) your property if you fail to make payments.
- Home equity loans: Equity means ownership. "Home equity" refers to the percentage of the property you personally own. If you've bought the property with cash, you have 100% equity. However, if you used a mortgage,

you'll have a certain percentage of equity based on how much you've already repaid. Fortunately, if you want to take another loan, you can opt for a Home Equity Line of Credit (HELOC) or Home Equity Loan.

- Home Equity Line Of Credit: HELOC loans are a type of revolving credit. This means you can withdraw from the line of credit whenever you need it and then repay it so that the line of credit is once again available to you in full. It works just like a credit card, only with a bigger amount. During the "draw period," you only pay interest against the amount you've borrowed. After this period lapses, you generally have around 20 years to repay the full amount. These types of loans have variable interest rates.

- Home Equity Loan: These are installment loans. You end up getting a lump sum in one go and then you're supposed to pay it back over a specific period as monthly installments. These have a fixed interest rate.

- Credit builder loans: These are designed to help people with very low or poor credit ratings get a chance to rebuild their scores. A specific amount—somewhere from $250 to $1,000—is deposited into some kind of savings account and you pay fixed monthly payments for anywhere between 6 months to 24 months. Once the loan is repaid, the lender returns the deposited money and reports all your transactions to credit bureaus so that your credit scores can be bumped up. However, before you do jump in, be sure that your lender does report to the credit bureau. Otherwise, this entire exercise will be in vain.

- Debt consolidation loans: These loans are designed to help people pay off high-interest debt. What they do is reduce your applicable interest rates, which helps you save money on existing debts. Not only that, the lender will also merge all loans into one so that you just have to pay one party instead of paying several. As a result of this, and the lower interest rate, you end up saving a fortune.

- Payday loans: This is a short-term loan that comes with a whopping 400% annual percentage rate (APR). This isn't the kind of loan that you want to apply for because you don't want to pay this high interest rate. I wouldn't even bother saying that these loans are designed to "help" because they are the type of loans you want to avoid at all costs.

- Small business loans: Entrepreneurs can use this type of credit service to tap into a sizable loan that can help them with their small business operations. From purchasing stock to handling payroll and more, entrepreneurs can use small business loans as a financial cushion, making day-to-day financial decisions easier, without having to put together a large amount of capital.

Should You Apply for a Loan?

Whether you need a loan or are thinking about applying for one, there are a few things worth remembering here.

Banks want to lend you money. They don't do it because they love you, or anyone else for that matter, but because that's how they make their money. They charge us interest and they can't do that unless we borrow some money from them.

Banks are always coming up with credit offers and schemes that can catch you off guard and compel you to apply. Once you do, you get an influx of money but then end up paying a lot more than you originally borrowed.

The good thing here is that you can't apply for most loans as a teenager without having your parent or grandparent co-sign. This may sound like a bad thing, but it really isn't. Thanks to years of experience and knowledge, your parents and family members will be able to guide you in the right direction. Something may look like a great deal to you but they can easily spot the red flags and let you know if it's a good deal or not. They can look into the loan and see if the terms and conditions are as friendly as the bank claims.

Besides, even if they do agree, the banks and lenders will carry out background checks, credit history, and so much more. What truly influences their decision to lend you money is what you intend to do with the money once they've loaned it to you. Other aspects, such as assets, income, and debts, will also play a role in helping banks decide what to do with your loan application.

Coming back to the original question: Should you get a loan? It depends. If things are dire and there is no other way out, perhaps. If it's just something you want, absolutely not. If you intend to buy yourself a property or a car, it can be a good idea. However, if you want to invest the loan money into something like stocks or bonds, it's best not to get a loan as investments can turn into losses. This will mean you'll end up owing more than you borrowed, and that's bad.

Never invest any amount of money that isn't yours. Make that a rule of life. With that said, if you still want to go for a loan, it's better to plan and prepare yourself for all sorts of questions that bankers may ask you before approving your loan application.

Think about how you're going to answer the bank or lender's questions, such as what you intend to do with the money, how you intend to repay the loan, how much you can afford to pay every month, and what your total income and expenses are. Prepare your answers beforehand to give yourself a fighting chance.

PRACTICAL STEPS TO BUILD AND MAINTAIN A POSITIVE CREDIT HISTORY

Since everything is about your credit history, it makes sense to learn how you can build and maintain a positive credit history.

Learn About Credit Basics

Start by learning what credit is, how it works, and how it can impact your financial future. If ever you need a reminder of the different terms, you can just go back to the section above as a refresher.

Become an Authorized User

Since only those who are 18 and older can apply for a credit card, consider becoming an authorized user on a family members credit card. They will need to inform the bank and go through the entire process but this will help you understand how credit cards work and how to be responsible. Take note that you'll need to be accountable for the purchases that you make through this credit card.

Open a Bank Account

Whether you open a checking account or a savings account, opening one helps you start building your credit history. It's a great way to show the credit bureaus that you're able to handle your money, save it, and utilize it effectively.

Get Yourself a Job

There's nothing better than finding a job that pays you. However, since you're just a teenager, you may only be offered a part-time job, but that's great too. Not only do you get to work and learn new things while earning money, but you also have enough time to focus on your studies. As you make money, you start learning more about the value of money. You'll find that you voluntarily reduce unnecessary expenses and focus on important ones when you use your own money.

Having an income stream will also help your credit history and is a good way to eventually secure yourself a credit card.

Pay All Your Bills On Time

I can't stress enough just how important it is to pay your bills on time. If it helps, note down the due dates for all your bills, rental payments, and any recurring bills. Note these dates down and make it a point to pay your bills before the due date. You want to do this for two reasons: first, to avoid additional charges and second, to avoid getting marked for late payments, which leads to a reduced credit score.

Obtain a Secured Credit Card

Generally, credit cards are unsecured, meaning that you don't put anything up as collateral. However, that leads to very high interest rates. A secured credit card, on the other hand, requires you or your family member to put down a deposit that serves as collateral. Once the deposit is made, a credit card is issued to the cardholder on the account. As long as you make your payments on time, you have nothing to worry about. If you fail to make your payments, the institution will claim your deposit as collateral.

Making payments on time helps you build a better credit report. Failure to make repayments can lead to negative results.

Consider Getting a Student Credit Card

This isn't a common credit card or one you can find easily. Student credit cards exist to help you responsibly build your credit. This has fewer requirements as well as lower credit limits. If you remain a good user, keep the utilization under a certain threshold, and make your payments on time, you're rewarded for your good financial behavior.

Tap Into a Credit Builder Loan

You can always opt for a credit builder loan, which works almost the same as secured credit cards. You deposit a certain amount, anywhere from $250 to $1,000, in a savings account or a certificate of deposit (CD). You simply continue to pay monthly payments until the loan is paid off.

Once you complete the payments, the money is returned to you— excluding the interest you paid—and your credit score is improved. This type of loan is used only to build credit.

Student Loans

I'm not exactly a fan of these, but if you're aiming for college, perhaps consider getting yourself a student loan. Remember, not all loans are bad. Just like a mortgage, which helps you build equity and net worth, student loans help you gain access to higher education which can then convert into high-paying career opportunities.

Explore all the ways to pay for college, including student loans. Ideally, you want to pay for it on your own. However, if you don't have the money to pay for college, consider getting a Federal student loan.

EXPERT ADVICE ON MANAGING STUDENT DEBT AND AVOIDING DEBT TRAP

If you decide to get a student loan, first make sure you're aware of what it involves. While everything may look simple and easy, you may end up with some unexpected challenges. If you end up signing up for the wrong college, the wrong kind of student loan, or agreeing to something you're not supposed to, you may find yourself in all sorts of financial trouble.

To help you get started with the student loan and ensure you manage it wisely, here are some expert tips to follow.

Make the Right Choice of School

Before you even apply for a student loan, you need to find a school. Not just any school; the perfect school. A school, college, or university that offers the program you want, has a good academic reputation and offers convenience. It must offer great benefits and opportunities, and it should do that without breaking your bank account. School fees and additional costs will be something important to consider.

Compare different institutions to find the one that ticks all the boxes, or most. Once you have the one you like, you can then move to the next step.

Only Borrow What You Need

If your course costs X amount of dollars, be sure to borrow exactly that. If you wish to borrow money to only cover your tuition and other associated fees, don't borrow an additional amount for your housing, transportation, and food. Ideally, you want to handle that part on your own while using the student loan to pay for your tuition and academic fees.

At no point are you required to borrow the maximum. The lending institute may try and sell you the idea of borrowing the entire amount because "There's no harm in having extra money," but remember not to fall for that. Doing so will only increase your monthly payments and burden you more than you can handle at the moment.

Look Like a Student, Live Like One as Well

Many students believe it's okay to be a student and have a luxurious lifestyle. They buy all the latest fashion, such as clothes, gadgets, watches and more. However, you want to avoid this money trap. That's money going down the drain that you'll never be able to recover. Instead, live like a student, and dress like one as well.

It may sound okay to grab a latte every day, but if you add up the cost, you'll end up spending thousands of dollars by the time you're done with your education.

Always Aim for Federal Loans

Aim for a federal loan over any private loans. Private lenders have strict terms and conditions and they often run background checks, including credit history checks. Federal loans, on the other hand, are more flexible when it comes to lower interest rates and flexible repayment options.

With that said, you need to be a degree candidate and formally admitted to a program to qualify for a federal student loan.

In case you can't find a federal loan and need to go for a private one, here are some steps you need to take before you apply for one:

- Do your research: Go through the terms and conditions carefully. Always seek assistance from family members and from others who have been down this road before, to help you learn from their experiences.
- Use a co-signer: Having a co-signer can help reduce the interest rates you'll pay, and will come with more favorable terms overall
- Look for alternatives: You can always ask your employer to see if they can give you tuition assistance. You can also look into scholarships and apply for the ones you're eligible for as these can greatly help reduce the financial burden.
- Look for deals: Many places offer student discounts on things such as transportation, housing, and food. Not only that, but you can also rent books instead of buying them, helping you save a lot of money in the process.
- Make payments early: While you're attending your classes, try and make your payments early. This prevents capitalization and helps keep the principal amount you owe lower and easier to manage.
- Ask for help: Financial aid offices are set up to help students like you gain more information and understand how the financial side of studying works. If you find

yourself stuck or unable to understand what to do next, get in touch with them and ask for help.

That's not all. Here are some additional tips for you to remember and use to repay your student loan easily:

- When possible, make extra payments towards your principal amount. This will help reduce the amount you owe in total.
- If you have a steady job and a good credit history, you can refinance your student loan to pay it off without worrying about any extra payments. Just like debt consolidation, this brings in all your student loans into one—if you have more than one loan—and offers a lower interest rate. This way you can also choose a new term—ideally less than what's left on your existing loans.
- Utilize autopay features. You can sign up for autopay, which will keep you on schedule for your payments automatically, and assures that you won't miss a payment.
- Aim to make bi-weekly payments instead of making a full payment every month. This will help you reduce your principal amount significantly and wrap your loan up faster.
- If you have capitalized interest, something that happens if you continue school and don't make any payments during the grace period, you'll have to pay a higher amount. Ideally, you want to avoid this. However, if you already have capitalized interest, pay that off first. If you make monthly or biweekly payments when the interest is accruing, you can avoid capitalization completely.
- If you can't make quicker payments, it's best to stick to the standard payment plan. In the case of Federal loans, you usually get a 10-year repayment plan. Stick to that. While

you can always opt for longer durations that offer smaller monthly repayments, it's best to stick to the standard term to pay your debt off quicker.

- Got yourself a bonus or some extra cash? Use that, or a portion of that, to pay off your debt. You can also use any money you earn from side hustles to make additional payments every time you get paid. This will speed up the repayment process and will translate into you paying your debt off sooner.

With that said, there's an elephant in the room that needs to be addressed; what if you don't want to use student loans? Is it even possible to fund your studies on your own? Well, it definitely is.

Tips to Avoid Debt Traps

For those who are aiming to avoid falling for debt traps and student loans, there are strategies and ways you can use to your advantage to give yourself the best possible chance of avoiding these.

Take Up Hybrid Learning

Hybrid learning is a new way of learning where you take some classes online while taking some on-campus. This offers flexibility and convenience. Not just that, it can also save you a fortune in the long run as you won't have to travel every day to attend your classes.

If you opt for hybrid learning, you'll find it far more affordable when compared to traditional on-campus learning. In some cases, you may even find the per-credit cost significantly lower than usual, meaning that your overall cost of education will reduce drastically.

Pay Cash for Education

Those who can pay cash are in the best situation possible to avoid debt at all costs. However, how do you get there?

Plan ahead and decide that you'll stick to paying by cash only. When you do that, you'll automatically start looking for ways to make more money, seek better alternatives, and find opportunities that you may have missed out on otherwise.

Choose Your Educational Institution Carefully

Be very careful when deciding on a school, college, or university. Unless you earn a scholarship, you can choose to explore options like a public, in-state institution that offers a four-year college program. These cost significantly less and still offer great chances at acquiring a degree.

If, however, you're aiming for private and prestigious universities, seek out ones that offer hybrid learning.

Transfer Your Credits

You can go to summer school at your local community college to rack up some credit to help you get into the institution of your choice more easily. Not just that, since you'll already have some credits, you won't need to take these courses again.

You can transfer those credits to your new school, and that will help you reduce your cost significantly.

Apply for Financial Aid

There are many scholarships, student aid programs, and grants that exist to help students. These are generally offered to students who are good at academics. These don't need to be paid back.

Start by filling out and submitting the Free Application for Federal Student Aid (FAFSA). Doing so will help FAFSA determine any grants or aid you qualify for, on both state and federal levels, as well as others.

Go for Test Out

If you have an exceptional command over a course that you're supposed to take, you can opt for "Test Out." These are essentially tests that see whether you have a firm grasp of the course. If so, you can be awarded credit for the course without ever taking a class.

Now, before you decide to jump and test out on all your courses, it's worth noting that these do have some costs. While it's significantly lower than taking the entire course, it's still a good idea to only go for these after you've prepared to the best of your abilities.

Find Work On Campus

Many colleges and universities offer on-campus work. Be sure to seek out such opportunities. Almost all on-campus work comes with many discounts and benefits. For example, from your sophomore year onwards you can become a Resident Advisor (RA) for your college dorm. As an RA you get hefty discounts on food as well as housing for as long as you remain in the school. As a result, you end up saving quite a lot of money.

Part-Time Jobs

On-campus work opportunities are good, but they may not pay that well. If that is the case, you can always opt for some part-time jobs that can help you not only gain experience but also make quite a lot of money. You can use that money to pay for your tuition, new courses, exams, and so on.

Discuss Repayment Plans

You can speak to your college about repayment plans and options. While you do have the choice to pay upfront for all your education, you can also negotiate some decent terms with your college and pay for your education over time. Colleges generally offer interest-free repayment plans, making this another great option.

CREDIT AND DEBIT CARDS

While we've vaguely talked about this earlier, it can still take some time to understand properly.

People, especially teenagers, often use the words credit and debit interchangeably. However, these are two completely different types of accounts. One is designed to lend you money and make money off you while the other is designed to allow you to use your own money and keep debts away.

A debit card is directly linked to your bank account. Therefore, if you have $1,000, you can use that at any given time and whatever amount you use will automatically be deducted from your account.

On the other hand, we have credit cards. The term "credit" is the giveaway here. This isn't your money, it belongs to the credit card issuer and they are only lending it to you. Even if you have $50 in your account and you have a credit card with a $1,000 credit limit, you can use up to $1,000 without worrying about your bank balance.

For debit cards, you don't need to make any repayments. Any deposit you make into your account is the amount that is available on your card. For credit cards, you need to repay the amount you borrow. Any repayment you make goes to paying the loan and any applicable interest.

A debit card can be a good tool if you use it properly and responsibly. Using these offers you the following benefits:

- Helps prevent increasing debt
- Allows you to pay right away and not worry about a bill later on
- Offers you immediate and easy access to cash

Every checking account generally comes with a debit card. A debit card will also have "debit card" written in most cases, to help differentiate between it and a credit card.

While there may be bad aspects to credit cards, they do offer some advantages. These include:

- Extra time to pay for your purchases
- Help in building a credit history
- Convenience for emergencies

There's no harm in applying for a credit card, as long as you make sure to use it responsibly. Credit card vendors push you to make the minimum payment, so they make more money. Be aware of this. It's okay to make the minimum payment once in a while, but don't make it a monthly habit. That's yet another debt trap that can put you in a never-ending debt cycle. Rather pay as much as you can.

When choosing a credit card, be sure that you have a decent credit score. You also want to ensure that you apply for credit cards that have lower interest rates and higher credit limits. The higher the credit limit, the more room you have to maintain a lower utilization rate.

Also, keep an eye out for any annual fees. Some credit cards come with an annual fee that you're liable to pay. You can use Google to help you search for the best deals available. Once you're happy with the terms and the credit limit, you can apply for your first credit card.

EXERCISE TIME - TEENS & PARENTS

For this exercise, it will involve both parents and teens.

Parents - if you give you children an allowance or pay them to complete certain chores around the house, this is the perfect time to teach them about lending.

When your teen asks you for an advance in their allowance, this is the perfect time to teach them about borrowing, lending, paying interest, and the principles of debt. Instead of asking them to do more chores around the house to earn more money, loan them the money. You'll sit down with your child, explain what the terms are of the loan, how much interest you'll be charging them, how much they'll pay over the life of the loan, etc. You can then ask them if they'd like to accept the loan given the terms of the agreement.

This is a great teaching moment for you and a great learning lesson for your teen.

Teens - Borrowing money from your parents may seem weird at first, but it's a common practice, and who better to start with than your parents. You can openly ask them questions about the loan process, why they would loan you money, what their profit looks like, and how they came up with fair terms.

CHAPTER 4

CRAFTING YOUR BUDGET MASTERPIECE

 Budgeting has only one rule: Do not go over budget.

LESLIE TAYNE

When you start making money, you need to know where your money is coming from as well as where it's going. It sounds somewhat obvious, but trust me on this one, you'd be surprised to learn just where your money can go.

Making money is the part everyone understands, but most fail to understand how to use it properly, which is one of the biggest reasons why people end up in debt. They don't know what their expenses are, nor do they have any idea how much money they are supposed to spend. They spend first and then worry later, a recipe for disaster.

To ensure that you don't follow that path, you'll learn something called budgeting. It's powerful, it's easy, and it can help transform your life for the better. Think about it like a superpower that grants you the ability to make future financial decisions more confidently.

HOW TO CREATE AND STICK TO A BUDGET

A budget is a financial document that shows you all your income sources, the amount you're earning, and all your expenses. It's a document that you can easily modify, update, or change completely to better suit your financial position.

A budget helps you understand all the sources you earn money from, including:

- Full-time jobs
- Part-time jobs
- Online gigs
- Side hustles
- Businesses
- Dividends
- Cash bonuses
- Gifts

It also takes into consideration all your expenses. These include:

- Food
- Transport
- Rent
- Utility bills
- Taxes
- Loans

The beauty of budgeting is that people of any age can understand this concept and create an easy-to-follow budget. Creating a budget is easy, and it brings a lot of financial maturity to the mix. Think about this as a plan that helps you know how to spend your money.

I know, it doesn't sound that great. However, if you stick to your budget, you'll be thanking me later because you'll end up saving quite a lot of money. You can then use that money to invest and make even more money.

Around 56% of teens have discussed or at least touched upon the topic of finances with their parents (Lake, 2022). Despite that, only a third of the people from the class of 2020 high school graduates actually had goals of being financially independent in the next 10 years (Lake, 2022). That's a very low number, and it's mostly because many don't understand what budgets can do.

Budgets can help us manage our finances and even meet our financial goals. A budget isn't necessarily all about spending. It helps you identify expenses that you can cut down on, create additional savings, and eventually meet your short-term and long-term financial goals.

So, how exactly do you create one? Well, let's learn.

Step-By-Step Guide to Crafting a Budget

There is no right or wrong in creating a budget. Your budget will differ from the next person as everyone has their own unique financial situation, income, and expenses. So, you can first learn how to create a budget and then explore better ways to tweak it to fit your specific requirements.

Step 1: Understand Your Income

The very first thing you want to do is to understand how much money you make. Any amount of money that comes your way is an income. This includes:

- Gifts
- Bonuses
- Tips
- Regular paychecks
- Part-time income
- Money from side hustles
- Profits from any businesses
- Dividends
- Money earned through freelancing
- allowances
- rental income (if applicable)

Write down each stream of income you get under the heading "Income." Be sure to write where this income is coming from. Once you have listed all your sources of income and their amounts, add them up.

It's important that you only include the sources of income that you're certain to make, not the ones you hope to make.

Once you've added all your income and have a total number, that's your total money in hand. Whatever your budget will be, it must match this number or be lower, in ideal circumstances.

Step 2: Start Tracking Your Expenses

Start by creating another heading named "Expenses." List down every expense here. Start with the ones that you know are certain and must be paid. These can include (if applicable):

- Rent
- Energy bill
- Water bill
- Mobile phone bill
- Internet bill
- Food
- Transport

The ones listed above are your needs as you can't function or live without them.

Once that's done, take note of every other expense that you have. A great way to ensure you don't miss out on expenses is to record the expense the moment it happens. You can download a variety of apps on your smartphone that can help you record and budget properly.

The goal here isn't to see how much you spend. It's to see where your money is going. Once you know that, you can then take control over how much of it goes where.

Step 3: Create Your Budget Categories

Now that you know all your income and expenses, it's time to organize them.

Create categories that can help manage things more effectively. It's very important to understand the difference between needs and wants if you want to do this correctly.

Not everything you want is what you need, and not everything you need is what you want. For example, you need food to live. Similarly, you need clothes, internet, gas, water, shelter, and so on. Your wants, on the other hand, are things like going to a concert, takeout, watching a movie, or buying something extravagant.

Place the things you need under relevant headings. Put the things you want under "discretionary spending." The goal is to know how much money goes into each of these categories and then work out ways to reduce your spending.

You can always create subcategories to help you further gain clarity. For example, under discretionary spending, you can have a category of "Money spent when with friends." You may spend money on food, travel, movies, or shopping when you're out with your friends. List such expenses under this subcategory.

Step 4: Work Out Where Your Money Is Going

Next, you need to start identifying where your money is going. It can take some time to work out the details as you've just started with this. Record every single expense, along with their amounts, under the right category. Do this the entire month and you'll easily find out where you spend the most money.

Once again, the goal is to cut down on expenses. For example, you need a place to live so you pay rent. That's understandable, but if it's a larger apartment than you need, it's more of a want. Perhaps consider moving into a smaller apartment with lower rent payments or sharing the apartment with others.

Remember, you're probably a student at this point in life. As a student, it's important to live like a student, not a millionaire. The aim is to find all the avenues where you can cut down your expenses. If you're ordering food from restaurants every day, consider cooking your own meals and packing lunch.

If a certain category shows a spike, look into it to find out where you were spending more during that period. A budget can help you better understand your financial situation but it can only offer information. How you act on that information is your call.

Ideally, you want to spend less than what you earn. At most, you can have a zero-balance budget where you end up spending exactly as much as you earn. While both approaches are good, the latter isn't what you aim for if you wish to save and later start investing.

Step 5: Time to Set Your Financial Goals

Setting both short-term and long-term financial goals is important. Make sure these are SMART goals, as we learned about in Chapter 2.

Let's say you wish to save up enough money to set up an emergency fund. You plan to set this up in the next two years to help you navigate through any unforeseen setback without worrying at all. To make it more attainable, you set your goal to $2,000. Now, you know that you want to find ways to generate this amount within this time frame.

Next, you can set long-term financial goals for yourself. These can be:

- Buying a house
- Investing in a rental unit or property

- Buying a used car
- Repaying all your debts
- Buying or starting your own business

Whether you set short-term or long-term goals, you can only ever achieve them by generating some savings. Therefore, if you haven't already done so, start cutting down expenses where possible. Stop spending unnecessarily, start living efficiently, and avoid falling for impulse buying.

Over time, your savings will grow, allowing you to not only achieve your smaller financial goals but your larger ones as well.

A great way to generate savings is to use the 50/30/20 rule for your budget. This is broken down as:

- 50% of your income is spent on all your needs. This includes your utility bills, rent, food, clothing, water, and transport costs.
- 30% of your income is allocated to your wants. This means that if you want to watch a movie, hang out with friends, go shopping, or buy something new, you use this money.
- 20% of your income must go straight into your savings. This may be hard at first, but instead of waiting the entire month, deposit 20% of your income into the bank right away. Better yet, set up an automatic transfer so that it happens automatically.

Step 6: Know Your Wants and Needs

As I mentioned earlier, needs and wants are two separate things. You need a place to live, but living in a luxurious place is a want. Similarly, you need clothes, but they don't have to be designer wear or trendy.

A good way to see if something is a need or a want is to ask yourself a few important questions before making a purchase. Based on the answers, you can determine what you're dealing with.

- Will this purchase help me improve my life?
- If I don't buy this, will it cause difficulties for me?
- Can I function properly without it?
- Are there cheaper alternatives that offer the same value?
- Can this wait?

These are some important questions worth considering. In most cases, what you think is a need will turn out to be a want, and that's not a mistake. That's just how we're forced to think. This is why marketing companies and big businesses make millions. They push products and services and make us feel like we need them.

Of course, not all wants are bad. If you want to eat out with your friends, that's perfectly fine. However, doing it every day or even every week will end up impacting your budget. Similarly, if public transport can get you to where you want to go, there's no need to drive a car. Save money on fuel and stick to using public transport.

Making these small moves will help improve your savings significantly. You may not see the results right away, but I assure you that you'll be surprised how they add up over time.

Step 7: Adjust Your Budget

Let's say you end up getting a raise. What do you do? Update your budget right away. If you lose your job, do the same. If you move to a new property, sign up for a new course, get additional gigs, or have any financial changes, update your budget right away.

Once the budget is updated and it's reflecting all the changes, focus on keeping track of your money just as before. Make adjustments where needed. For example, you may find that allocating $500 to discretionary spending may be too much. Reduce that to $400. You end up saving $100 in addition to what you were saving before. If your rent has gone up, make the changes to your budget.

Don't wait to see how the new changes will affect your financial situation. Update the budget and the result will become obvious.

Step 8: Stick to Your Budget

The last step is to stick to your budget. Be sure to allocate your money properly. Track all your expenses. Keep checking your bank statements to find out any hidden fees or unnecessary charges. If you spot these, such as a subscription that you don't even use anymore, cancel it and make some additional savings. Every penny counts because it's all going to play some role in the future.

TOOLS AND APPS TO SIMPLIFY BUDGETING

Budgeting can be intimidating, especially for teenagers. Since you're doing it for the first time, you'd probably be worried about getting it wrong. Fortunately, there are two things here worth knowing:

- There's no such thing as a wrong budget. If you can't work with a budget, you just need to make adjustments to find one that fits better.
- There are many tools and apps you can use to help simplify the entire process.

To help you along, here are some great tools and apps that you can use to make your budgeting journey easier. These are all available to anyone under 18.

- *GoHenry*: A great app designed purely for budgeting purposes.
- *Revolut*: Another great app that helps teenagers create and modify budgets on the go.
- *BusyKid*: A great app for those looking to enhance their financial knowledge while making budgets, creating savings, and giving back.

Here are some free tools worth looking into:

- *The Budget Planner*: An app created by the Government of Canada.
- *MyDoh*'s budget savings calculator: Use this to know how much you'll end up saving.
- *MyDoh*'s free budget worksheets: There are many that you can download, modify, and use. Great for those starting with their budgeting journey.

EXERCISE TIME - TEENS & PARENTS

For this chapter, you'll start with a template budget sheet. You can modify it to your liking or search for budget templates online to find one that suits you better. However, this budget sheet is simple and easy and can help you get started properly. This exercise is for teens, but parents are welcome to use this template if you'd like.

Income

Income Source	Planned Amount	Actual Earned

Expenses

Expenses	Planned Amount	Actual Spent	Leak or Leftover

Savings

Planned Savings	
Leftover Money Not Spent	
Actual Money Put Into Savings	
Money Carry Over for Next Budget	

Like I said before, the entire goal of a budget is to help you understand where your money is coming from, and where it's going, and then help you identify how you can save it. Once you start saving, you can then start using that amount to achieve your short-term and long-term goals.

Speaking of savings, let's move on to the next chapter and learn some great strategies to help you save more.

MAKE A DIFFERENCE WITH YOUR REVIEW

UNLOCK THE POWER OF FINANCIAL FREEDOM FOR TEENS AND PARENTS

Over the years, I've seen far too many teens and parents struggle with financial literacy, and I'm on a mission to change that. But I can't do it alone. I need your help.

Please help that person who has yet to learn the concepts in this book by leaving a review on Amazon.

Would you be willing to lend a hand to a fellow teen or parent in need? It won't cost you a dime and takes less than a minute of your time.

Here's how you can make a difference:

Your review might seem small, but it will have a huge impact. It could help a struggling teen or parent:

- Start their journey towards financial freedom
- Start their own business
- Find meaningful work
- Transform their life

And your generosity will likely come back to you someday.

So, are you in? Are you ready to help your peers gain the financial knowledge they need to succeed?

If so, scan that QR code and leave a review. It's that simple.

Thanks for taking action, and remember, together we can make a difference.

Your friend in financial freedom,

Greg Junge

PS - Spread the wealth! If you think this book could benefit someone you know, pass it along. Sharing knowledge is the ultimate gift.

CHAPTER 5
THE SAVING ADVENTURE AWAITS

Wealth is not about having a lot of money; it's about having a lot of options.

CHRIS ROCK

Saving is hard, but it's well worth it. Having that extra bit of money in a savings account, or better yet invested where it continues to grow, pays off in the long run.

Whatever your financial goals are, everything starts with you saving money. Once you start saving, you can:

- Invest into stocks
- Deposit savings into a high-yield savings account
- Buy assets that make you money
- Buy a car
- Buy a house
- Go on a vacation

Whatever it may be, it starts with you saving money. Since it's that important, it's a great idea to learn some unique ways through which you can really amp up your savings and achieve your financial goals sooner.

INNOVATIVE WAYS TO SAVE MONEY

These apply to everyone, regardless of how much you may be earning. Saving is easy and simple if you know what you're doing and you stick to a plan.

You can save money in almost every situation. If you're someone who prefers to spend first and then save whatever you can in the end, you can find ways to cut costs and enhance your savings. If you're someone like me who takes a chunk of the income and puts it into a savings account first before deciding to spend the rest of it, you'll save a lot more.

Regardless of your saving style, here are some effective ways you can save more money and see your savings grow.

Micro Saving

Micro saving is quite literally saving tiny amounts of money frequently. For example, you have 50 cents that you managed to save. What do you do with it? You save it! I know it sounds odd. How can 50 cents help you with savings? Here's something I want you to calculate.

If you save 50 cents a day, for the next 365 days, you'll end up saving an additional $182.50. Continue doing this for the next five years, and you'll have a total savings of $912.50 just by saving those 50 cents a day, and that's not including using compound interest. Let's make this more interesting.

Let's say you have some extra dollars you managed to save. Perhaps you got paid a bonus, found additional gigs online, or received money as a gift from your parents or grandparents for your birthday. Don't waste it. Instead, add it to your savings.

For this example, let's assume you ended up with the following additional sum of money in year one:

1. $500 - Bonus from work
2. $250 - Part-time job savings
3. $400 - Birthday money from parents or grandparents
4. $600 - Online gig earnings that you never used

In total, you have $1,750. Let's also assume this is the average extra income you get every year for the next five years. Where do you think the savings account stands after five years?

$1,750 x 5 = $8,750

Add in the $912.50 you also saved by saving just 50 cents a day and you get **$9,662.50**.

Do you see how micro-saving works? What may appear tiny and almost negligible at the start can become something big, when done consistently. Yes, it takes time, but almost $10,000 in just five years is beyond impressive.

You can also open a specialized micro savings account with various financial institutions. These are designed to help you save every penny, earn interest while you do, and keep your savings separate from your spending money. The number we had before will certainly increase since we haven't taken into account the interest your savings would have earned by then.

Micro-saving is great, but it isn't the only way to save. What if you want to micro-save while finding ways to save even more? Well, I have quite a few answers to that.

Creative Ways to Save Money

Here are my top ways to help you save more money:

- Stop or cancel subscriptions you no longer use. You may be surprised to learn just how much money you've been paying for that gym membership or online gaming subscription that you haven't even used, or the streaming service you signed up for and never used again.
- Know and stick to your budget. While this can be challenging at times, try your best to stick to your budget. This will greatly help reduce costs and improve savings.
- Reduce energy consumption. Whether it's cold or hot outside, try and minimize your electricity use inside. Energy bills often upset your entire budget as they can get out of control quickly. Whenever you're leaving a room, turn off the appliances you can, the lights, and any other devices that are no longer in use. Don't turn all the lights on. Use one or two bright ones and turn them off as soon as you leave. Also, watch out for vampire devices. These are devices that are turned off, but they continue to use little electricity even while they are not functioning. The best way is to unplug these devices. Finally, use energy-saving lights and fixtures.
- Consider lowering your expenses. The rule of thumb suggests that you use no more than 30% of your income to handle housing expenses. If you have a higher rent payment, perhaps consider getting a roommate. For minor

repairs, do them yourself. If all else fails, move to a smaller or cheaper apartment.

- You can also talk to credit companies and negotiate a lower interest rate.
- Start eating at home. This may sound cumbersome, especially considering that you'll need to cook, but it really helps save a lot of money. Besides, you can cook whatever you want to eat. Not only can it be healthy and delicious, but it also makes economic sense.
- Always shop with a list. We tend to walk into the store thinking we know exactly what we want. In the end, we end up with a cart full of things we didn't need in the first place. This leads to extra spending. To overcome this, create a list of things that you need, and stick to that list when you're shopping.
- Stick to cash only. This may sound odd but when you carry cash, you know you can't go over the sum. If you do, you'll have to walk back home, grab more cash, and then come back. That's a lot of work.
- Pay off all or most of your debts. Doing so will free up a lot of additional money that you can then save right away.
- Buy used when and where possible. Instead of paying a high price for a new car, new pair of shoes, or even clothes, hop into thrift stores or go online and find used items. For vehicles, check online and ask someone you know who has experience in this area. Doing so will help save a ton of money.
- Many grocery stores have apps that allow you to save money by using digital coupons.

HOW TO START SAVING

While everyone wants to save money, most will be wondering "How do I get started?" Well, there's something called a 30-day savings challenge. It serves as a great starting point for teenagers and adults alike.

Challenge yourself to save for 30 days straight. You can save 50 cents, or you can save more than that if you want to challenge yourself. It doesn't matter what amount you save; what matters is that you saved something; this builds the habit of saving!

This takes some practice and patience. However, if you do this right, you'll end the 30-day challenge with some money to spare. Want to make things more interesting? Go for the 52-week challenge.

The 52-week challenge is just like the boss level of a game. Here, the idea is to start saving just 25 cents in the first week. In the next week, you add another quarter to it (that's another 25 cents) and save 50 cents. In the third week, you save 75 cents, and on and on. Do this correctly and you'll end up saving $344.50 by the end of the year.

Saving is a habit, not a concept. It's a habit that grows with time. Think of it like a baby learning how to walk. Sure, the baby crawls, falls, and tumbles but eventually learns how to walk because they grew in the habit of using their legs to walk. Now, we walk without even thinking about it, let alone putting any effort into it. Why? Because we're used to it. It has become a part of our daily lives. Similarly, when you start saving money, you start developing a habit. Over time, that habit becomes a part of who you are. This means you'll be saving money without putting in any extra effort.

To help you push those savings up, throw in a "no spending week" in the mix once a month. The goal of this week is to avoid spending any money at all. Of course, this does not mean you go past your due dates on rent, utilities, and bills. You'll still have to pay those, but you won't get to spend any additional money on yourself. Therefore, you won't:

- Buy tickets for a movie
- Eat out at a restaurant
- Go shopping
- Buy makeup
- Buy video games
- Buy a new subscription
- Spend money on leisure activities

This week may be hard, but the results will more than justify themselves.

Additional Ways to Save Money

Here are some additional ways you can save money.

- Create a buying plan for yourself. This buying plan helps you to think and do your research. No longer are you required to buy something blindly. Instead, you'll need to start looking for alternatives. As you do, you'll start buying things that offer the same value but cost less and, as a result, you'll start saving money.
- Start practicing how to do your grocery shopping. Grocery shopping isn't easy. The fact is that there is so much that you have to do, buy, and look for. Then, there is the trouble of giving in to impulse and buying something that wasn't on the list at all. The only way you can learn how to

control your impulses and buy the things you need is to practice.

- Start discovering jobs that pay you. There are loads of resources online. Use any you please and start searching for all the job titles and types you think are interesting. Find out which job pays the most, which has the most benefits, and which job has the most and least competition. Think about the jobs you'd like to do one day and then find out whether the numbers motivate you to pursue a career in that direction. Work out how long it will take to buy yourself a home, pay off any remaining debts, and lead a financially healthy life.
- Focus on needs now. We all "want" to buy this and that, but do we really have to? If you want a future where you're financially independent and secure, you need to let go of your wants for now and focus only on your needs.

One more thing you need to learn about that can help you save a fortune is impulse buying. I've been using this term for a while now, but it's time for us to look into what I really mean when I say impulse buying.

The Trap That Is Impulse Buying

Impulse buying can be a bigger problem than most realize. What is impulse buying? It's when you decide to buy something because it just happened to catch your attention. You buy it without thinking things through and later realize it was a mistake.

Thanks to the rise of social media, we are now facing problems that probably didn't exist before. While impulse buying isn't a new thing, it has taken center stage in the era of social media. Now, more than ever before, companies use strategic marketing campaigns to push products your way based on your interests, browsing history, information, purchase habits, and likes on social media.

In 2022, a survey was commissioned by a renowned entity Slickdeals. Surprisingly, a whopping 73% of the respondents reported that most of their purchases turned out to be unplanned (Rivera, 2023). An average person is said to spend around $314 every single month on impulse buying. This means they end up burning away over $3,600 a year.

Impulse buying isn't just limited to adults either. Teenagers are also caught in this whirlpool. As a result, they burn through their savings and are left back to square one.

To really amp up your savings, start combating the idea of buying anything impulsively. To help you with that, use the 30-day rule. If you find something that you want to buy, note it down and wait for the next 30 days. In most cases, your impulse will fade away in 30 days and you'll move on, saving quite a bit of money. However, if you still have the need to buy it, perhaps try and find alternatives.

EXERCISE TIME - TEENS & PARENTS

Here's another great exercise to help you get started with your savings. This exercise uses the popular Savings Jar/Account Challenge. Parents can help their teens with this exercise to help set up the account if needed, and also to help review the financials once the savings start to accumulate.

The challenge is simple:

1. Find and designate a jar of your choosing for savings. You can also do this with a savings account if you prefer.

2. Label this jar/account with the appropriate goal you wish to achieve using these savings.
3. Add money to the jar/account every week.
4. Don't withdraw from the jar/account.
5. Review how much is in your jar/account and watch it grow.

Remember, your savings are a starting point to something bigger and something significantly more rewarding. It's by generating savings that you can invest your money into something that helps you generate profit, possible passive income, and dividends. Let's see how you can use your savings and passions, and turn them into more money. After all, who wouldn't like to make more money without doing much?

CHAPTER 6
TURNING YOUR PASSIONS INTO PROFIT

 The future belongs to those who believe in the beauty of their dreams.

ELEANOR ROOSEVELT

History is brimming with success stories, one after the other, of inspiring people who believed in their dreams.

Dreaming big is great, but you need to know how to convert that dream into a reality. The best way to do that is to follow your passion. Have a passion for photography? Go for it. Come up with innovative techniques, new technology, or anything that helps solve a problem and offers assistance to other photographers. Be an entrepreneur and lead by example and I assure you that fortune will find you.

THOSE WHO DID IT

I can write an entire book about the people who have accomplished the impossible and cemented their names and legacy in history books. However, to keep things short, I'll introduce you to some of the most inspiring success stories of all time.

The Kid That Drew History

Back in the early 1900s, a kid developed a passion for drawing animated figures. He had a passion for drawing cartoon characters and they were of high quality. In fact, by the time he was 18, he landed a decent job as a cartoonist. However, soon it was evident that he wanted to do more. Besides, the company that hired him didn't really believe his cartoons were as effective.

Soon, he started his own company. Today, almost a century later, that company is one of the most well-known and beloved companies on the planet, Disney. That kid was none other than Walt Disney himself.

The Million-Dollar Blog

Michelle Schroeder-Gardner started her blog while she was busy pursuing her MBA. She named it Making Sense of Cents. While her education was important, she had a passion for writing and helping others. Little did she know that her blog would go on to explode in popularity.

In a very short span, she was able to pay off her entire student debt. Not just that, she and her husband quit their jobs and started traveling the world. Why? Her blog started making around $100,000 every month.

Her blog became the center of attention and added to her business:

- online classes
- affiliate marketing
- company-sponsored ads
- display ads (Schmohe, 2021)

Needless to say, a simple passion proved to be far more valuable than what she could have ever imagined. Today, her story motivates the world to pursue their dreams and never stop believing.

From No One to the Richest Man on Earth

In 1996, Jeff Bezos started an online company in his garage called Amazon. The idea was that this would serve as an online bookstore for people. The Internet wasn't that popular yet, but it was catching on. Not only did the internet catch on, but he ended up expanding his business faster than anyone could have imagined.

Today, Amazon is everywhere. We depend on it to buy products, books, and so much more. As of 2020, Jeff Bezos was listed as the richest man on earth (Schmohe, 2021).

The Mother of Three

Alicia Shaffer has a passion for fashion. As a mother of three, she started creating her own designs while working in the kitchen. She would sell her designs on Etsy, an online platform, and she did really well with her business. However, with time, her designs grew in popularity and were soon sought-after.

Soon, she was Etsy's biggest seller and was netting anywhere from $60,000 to $80,000 every month. With such success, she eventually left Etsy in 2015 and started her own business. That business earns over a million dollars every year.

The Rental Empire

While at university, Harvard Business School alumni, Jennifer Hyman and Jennifer Fleiss started buying dresses for parties, weddings, and other formal events in their sizes. They would go to different campuses and then rent those dresses out to other students, who didn't want to pay a fortune for a dress they'd only wear once or twice. While they were already working part-time, it wasn't paying much. This was one way they thought they'd make money and lighten their own wardrobes.

Today, their company is valued at over $1 billion. A passion for clothes turned into a business that can support them for life, and provide value to others who need and want their services.

The Story of Mrs. Fields

Debbi Fields had an interest in baking. Back in the late 1970s, she was a housewife. Her husband was the breadwinner of the house and had a good career as an economic consultant. While things were good, she felt like she could still make some extra money on the side.

She loved and knew how to bake well, and the market was ripe for the taking. Pursuing her passion, she started using her skills and developed a healthy part-time business. Her husband was sure nothing would ever come of it.

Today, her net worth stands at over $200 million and her cookies are a household name (Schmohe, 2021).

The Magical Pillow Pets

Jennifer Telfer is a mother of two. Her son loved the idea of sleeping with stuffed animals. This was a problem as these were very bulky. After much deliberation, she finally decided to do something about it.

Telfer ended up creating pillow pets. She took out a little under $1,000 from her savings account and invested it in creating an unusual and innovative pillow design. She then sold these to her friends and family members. Soon, this caught on. She started getting more orders and she continued delivering them to customers.

Today, Pillow Pets is known as one of the most successful brands that started as nothing more than a hobby, with an estimated value of over $100 million.

Looking Good

Spanx is yet another success story. Founded by Sara Blakely, this company became so popular that even Oprah Winfrey has spoken about it. It went on to become one of the most popular undergarment brands in existence.

Today, her net worth is at a staggering $610 million (Schmohe, 2021).

All of these success stories aren't just stories. They all have something to offer to us all, hope. Dreaming big is required for success at all levels, which makes achieving those dreams possible. These people have proven that if you believe in yourself and really set out to pursue your passion and put in the effort, you're likely to become a success story yourself.

HOW TO MONETIZE YOUR HOBBIES

The big question here is how. How do you monetize your hobbies, dreams, and passions? Well, here's a step-by-step guide to help you do just that.

1. Know and love your passions. Embrace it wholeheartedly. Whether you love gaming, traveling, cooking, or even reading, cherish every moment of it. Don't worry about what someone else will say. You'll always find people who share your passion and won't only help you achieve your dreams, but also make the journey much more enjoyable.

2. Identify and establish your niche. Every hobby has one. Figure out where your hobby or passion lies. Do your research and learn all about it. Find out what kind of people follow this niche, who they are, and what they do, and learn from other success stories. Knowing your niche is critical to your success because this is where you'll find your audience.

3. Start building your online presence. Let the world know who you are, what you stand for, what you offer, and what you love doing. For this, use social media, set up a blog, or create a YouTube channel. Remember, pay attention to your niche and audience. Ideally, you want to think like your audience because you're in that same audience.

4. Keep posting consistently. This is important. If you're someone who posts some content, like a video or a blog post, once in a blue moon, you're not going to find any success. Instead, aim for consistency. Plan ahead and know what you'll be posting, when, and where. Everything

comes down to your content. The more frequently you post, the more people get to know you. Your content must provide tips, information, success stories, and ideas, and help answer people's questions. Get this mix right and people will start following you.

5. Harness the power of social media. Use platforms like Instagram, TikTok, Meta, X, and others to further boost your reach. Set up pages and accounts and connect with your audience.

6. Monetize. You can do this in a few ways, or all of them if you want:

   A. Affiliate marketing: You can partner with another brand and sell their products through your channel. The more you sell, the bigger the commission. Be sure to provide honest insights to your audience so that they know what to expect if they buy the product, and stick to products that you genuinely like and use yourself. Promoting products just to make money isn't something I'd recommend from a personal values point of view, but that decision is ultimately up to you.

   B. Digital products: If you can, offer your audience digital products that they can buy. These include ebooks, patterns, designs, NFTs, or guides.

   C. Sell courses online: Whatever skills you have, help others learn by teaching them. Set up an online course, record your lectures or tutorials, and then sell that online course to your audience.

   D. Ad revenue: One of the most sought-after ways of making money is through displaying ads. As your channel, blog, or social media account grows in popularity, more people will start following you. This will certainly appeal to marketers and advertisers who wish to sell products and services related to your niche.

Once you've monetized, you'll start making money. However, the journey doesn't end there. Here are a few more things you can do to ensure a continuing and successful journey:

- Continue to engage with your community by responding to messages, emails, and comments.
- Be sure to diversify your income streams. You can do this by expanding your content and adding new layers, such as videos on YouTube, streaming, and other formats.
- Be patient. Sometimes it takes quite a while before you start seeing that first dollar roll into your account.
- Always believe in yourself. Don't let anyone else tell you what you can or can't do. If you believe strongly in something, you can certainly achieve your dream.

Becoming an entrepreneur isn't easy. Whether you're doing something online or working out of an office, your entrepreneurial journey is full of challenges. There are ups and downs, failures and successes. All of that is a part of the journey an entrepreneur goes through. Never fear failure. If anything, failure is your first step to success. Take every failure as a learning opportunity and fuse what you learned from that failure to avoid repeating that mistake and improve upon your idea for a better result.

Why Become an Entrepreneur

Of course, you could argue that you can study hard, find a great job that pays six figures a year, and lead a happy life, but remember, at the end of the day, you have a boss to report to.

Being an entrepreneur means leading your own team and pursuing your own vision.

When you're working at a company, you're working to help someone else obtain and achieve their goals and visions and help them grow successful.

If you start your own venture, you not only get an opportunity to grow as a person, but you also get to be a leader. You get to lead by example, set benchmarks for others, and learn. With time and perseverance, you start getting closer and closer to your vision. There will be ups and downs, and you may sometimes feel like it's best to quit, but that's where you know you're near a major breakthrough.

Entrepreneurs like Elon Musk didn't find success instantly. It took him years before he was able to break the barriers and find something that could help the masses and provide him with significant profits. The same is the case with Sir James Dyson, the man who invented the world's first bagless vacuum cleaner.

Another example is that of a teenager who found financial freedom, the story of Bella Tipping. She was just 12 when she dreamt of the idea of a platform, quite like Trip Advisor, which was tailored for kids. The idea was to have a platform where kids can learn more about vacation spots that are genuinely fun for kids, she created Kidzcationz.com.

Supported by her parents, she created the website that took off. Today, she continues to lead as an example of what teens can do when they follow their passions.

The difference between a business owner and an entrepreneur is their vision. A business owner seeks profits by working on pre-existing business models. An entrepreneur seeks out gaps in the market and tries to come up with something that has never been done before, or improve upon a product or service that already exists.

Therefore, it should come as no surprise that entrepreneurs are usually the ones who go on to find financial freedom, a state where you can fulfill all your needs and wishes without ever worrying about money. You can buy nice things if that's your goal, travel the world, give back to charities that you believe in, and help others who aren't as fortunate as yourself. These rewards can be a mix of many things, depending on your ultimate purpose or your motivation.

So, when do you start? Technically, now is a great time. If you start your entrepreneurial journey as a teenager, you can learn significantly more and gain a lot more success than those who start their entrepreneurial journeys later on in life.

You'll learn through experience, mentors, networking with the right people, your mistakes and your successes, other people's mistakes and failures, as well as books and videos. You'll also learn how to:

- Use and enhance your financial skills
- Manage time
- Express your creativity
- Develop your resilience and grit

The last one is very important. You need resilience and grit to help you get through the tougher phases of being an entrepreneur. You'll hit a lot of obstacles and barriers, but never let those run you down and demotivate you. Instead, find ways to work through them and you'll find success on the other end.

For many people, the biggest prize is financial freedom. If your entrepreneurial journey is a success, you end up making a lot more money than you can in an entire lifetime of working for someone else. Why? Because not only do you bring something new to the market, but you're also providing services that can help improve lives and solve problems. Needless to say, you end up being rewarded for that.

Financial independence is a point in life where you're no longer dependent on people, like your parents, or a specific source of income, like a job. You'll have the ability to do what you want, when you want, with whom you want, all while not stressing out about your finances. You'll have several income streams that continue to provide you with all the financial support you need.

Financial independence helps you achieve:

- Your saving goals
- A strong credit history
- Freedom to make decisions of your own
- A stress-free life
- An early retirement

"Is it difficult to become financially independent?"

That depends on your definition of difficult. Better questions to ask yourself are: How badly do I want it? Why do I want it so badly? Two things play an important role here. If you really want to be financially independent, you need to:

- Let go of the things you want for a while and cut down on expenses as much as humanly possible. This means no more eating out or shopping just because you feel like it.
- Finding additional sources of income. These can be additional jobs, side hustles, businesses, investments, and others.

It's not easy to become financially independent and it requires you to have a lot of grit, resilience, passion, commitment, and a strong will. However, there are many success stories, including those of teenagers, who have achieved financial freedom. What's stopping you from being the next success story and living a life you've dreamed of?

How to Set Up Your Own Business

It isn't what you do that matters; it's how determined you are and how clear you are about what you intend to do. I would encourage you to do what you enjoy when setting up a business. If you enjoy the work, you'll have a lot more fun and more likely more success as well.

Setting up a business may sound hard, but it really isn't. You just need to know what you're doing. To help you with that, here's a small step-by-step roadmap to get you started.

The following will vary depending on the business you decide to start or buy, so this isn't a one-size-fits-all list. One thing that I will emphasize strongly: Utilize the people and relationships around you to help you do this. Asking for help at any stage of business is a strength, not a weakness.

If you have the right people advising you, you'll save yourself a lot of time, money, and headaches, while increasing your rate and chances of success.

1. Come up with your business concept. Think about what your business offers, what makes it unique, and the value that it provides to others.
2. Learn more about your competition and market. Find out more about the leading players, what they are doing, the

demand in the market, and the average selling price, and note down all of this data.

3. Create your own business plan with this information.
4. Choose to set up as a sole proprietor, partnership, or limited liability company (LLC).
5. Register your business within your state and with the IRS to get the necessary licenses, taxation numbers, and approvals.
6. Get all your finances in order. If you have someone else investing, be sure to have the money ready.
7. Start funding your business to start producing products or offering services.
8. Get business insurance. It can often come to your rescue if you suffer any unforeseen loss.
9. Be sure you have all the right business tools you need to make things work the way you want
10. Start marketing your business on social media websites and through Pay-Per-Click (PPC) ads.
11. Once the orders are coming in nicely, start scaling your business. Add in more products or services, hire more people, and grow your brand.

Before you go ahead, it's important to consider whether you want to partner with anyone or do things on your own. If you're bringing in a partner, be sure they are someone you can trust, someone who shares your vision, and is available. If you have passive investors (silent partners), don't expect them to work at all as they are only interested in funding your business and reaping profits, leaving you to tackle all the work. Regardless of the route you take, be sure to consider things thoroughly before inviting others to be your partners and investors.

EXERCISE TIME - TEENS & PARENTS

For this exercise, we will be using something called a SWOT Analysis worksheet. Parents and teens can work together on this, as this exercise takes a lot of critical thinking. The more complex the challenge, the better it is to have more brainpower in the room.

The SWOT stands for Strengths, Weaknesses, Opportunities, and Threats. This worksheet will help you understand where you are and how you can make better business decisions.

Before you start, you need to:

- Write your business idea down at the very top of the sheet
- Divide the paper into four sections, one for each of the SWOT components
- List down your answers in bullet points
- Review your answers
- Find ways to use your strengths and opportunities to overcome threats and weaknesses

For each of the four components, we will have some questions. The goal is to answer those questions and understand if a decision is good or bad.

Strengths:

- What advantage does your business have?
- What is it that you do better than anyone else?
- What unique resources can you use or have that others don't?

Weaknesses:

- What can you improve within the business?
- What is it that you should avoid doing?
- What are people likely to see as a weakness?

Opportunities:

- What good opportunities can you spot?
- What kind of trends are you aware of?
- Is there a gap in the market that you can fill?

Threats:

- What challenges do you face?
- What is your competition doing?
- Do you have any such weakness that can directly threaten your own business?

Investors and entrepreneurs do SWOT analyses all the time. It's one of the best ways to ensure you don't end up making a bad decision.

Speaking of investors, it's time we move on to the next chapter and learn more about the complexities of the financial system and investing so that you can learn how to make things work in your favor.

CHAPTER 7
CRACKING THE FINANCIAL CODE

 An investment in knowledge pays the best interest.

BENJAMIN FRANKLIN

The biggest mystery that many teenagers struggle with is: Why do some people manage to make money almost effortlessly while others are grinding hard to make a meager paycheck?

All this time, the answer's been right there in front of us. It's all about understanding the financial system and its complexities that can massively tilt the scales in your favor. This is why those who learn and understand financial literacy end up making money effortlessly whereas most continue living paycheck to paycheck, complaining about how unfair life is. Let's change that!

HOLISTIC APPROACH TO UNDERSTANDING THE FINANCIAL SYSTEM

Some of the terms may sound complex or intimidating but don't worry, I'll explain all that you need to understand.

A financial system is defined as "an economic arrangement wherein financial institutions facilitate the transfer of funds and assets between borrowers, lenders, and investors" (Johnson, 2021). Let's make some sense of that.

Think of the entire financial system as a way of dealing with money that's accepted by all banks and institutions. It's easy to use, easy to manage, and easy to monitor. Through this, anyone can buy and sell assets as well as receive and send money. Since money is involved, banks can also lend money, borrowers can borrow money, and investors can invest their money.

Financial markets are made up of lenders, investors, borrowers, banks, credit unions, et cetera.

We also have central planners who make decisions for the system and us. They decide where the funds go, who will receive the funds, and then who will manage them. This is where you'll need business managers or representatives from both sides.

A typical financial system has a bit of both. With that said, let's look into the components that make up a financial system.

Financial Institutions

These include all such financial organizations where you can acquire a variety of goods and services. This is where borrowers meet lenders and vice-versa. These institutions provide important services, such as reinsurances, foreclosures, and other brokered services.

The purpose of these institutions is to help mobilize money, and savings, and raise cash from other capital instruments.

Financial Markets

Financial markets, in proper terms, are places where trading takes place. This is where you can buy and sell things, such as stocks. NASDAQ, the popular name within the stock market, is just one of many examples.

Money

No financial system is complete without money. Money is the foundation upon which the entire system is built.

Financial Services

These include services like:

- Investing
- Banking services offered through liabilities
- Healthcare
- Investment management

Financial Instruments

Anything that can be bought by money and sold for money falls in this category. These include:

- Mortgages
- Contracts
- Equities
- Shares
- Premiums

Financial Regulatory Bodies

With all this money involved, the system needs a body that governs fairness and transparency and has the authority to intervene when things look suspicious. This is where central banks come in. Their job is to provide financial assistance to the country. However, central banks don't manage things. That part is handled by the government and other institutions. Since this topic is vast and quite complicated, I won't be taking much of your time on this for now.

Functions of Financial Systems

Financial systems "enable the smooth and secure transfer of funds between individuals, businesses, and institutions. They provide payment systems, such as electronic funds transfer, credit cards, and digital wallets, which facilitate the settlement of transactions and support economic activities." (Gowtham, 2023).

Types of Financial Services

There is a range of financial services to choose from. Here are some commonly used financial services that you can learn more about:

- Real estate investing services
- Mutual funds: A type of investment option that allows numerous investors to participate, invest, and collect mutual profits. A professional manages these so that it's done properly and monitored around the clock.
- Banking
- Wealth management
- Advisories: Financial advisors provide valuable insights based on extensive research.

I know that the financial world can sound slightly complicated, but it's a good idea to learn as much as you can about it. This helps you understand how things work, why investors make certain decisions, and how events such as natural disasters and pandemics impact the overall financial system.

Please be aware that some of the services listed above are salespeople first, meaning that you should always be aware of what's in it for them when engaging with their services.

The Power of Compound Interest

Now, let's talk about making some money the good old-fashioned way.

So far, I've been saying over and over again that you need to save money. You already know how to do that. However, what do you do when you've saved money? How do you make use of your savings so that it starts to grow over time?

Well, one way is to deposit all your savings into a savings account. When you continue doing that, you'll start earning interest on your savings over time. The bigger the amount you deposit, the bigger the return. However, a traditional savings account never pays too much.

At the time of writing this book, the average interest rate for a savings account in the US was around 0.46% (Knueven, 2024). That's pathetic. However, there's something called a high-yield savings account.

These have significantly more returns. You can earn around 5% to 7% return a year. Once again, that isn't enough. What do you do if you really want to change things and make a fortune over time? Well, that's where compound interest comes in.

Generally speaking, banks pay you interest based on the principal amount you deposit. This means that if you deposited $1,000 in the bank, you'll receive interest only on that $1000.

Compound interest, on the other hand, allows you to earn interest on top of the interest you've already earned. How? Let me explain using simple math.

Let's say you deposit $1,000 into a savings account that has a return of 10%. By the end of the first year, you'll have $1,100 in your account. The next year, you'll still make 10%, but not on the initial $1,000. Instead, you'll be making it on $1,100. This will continue until you've decided to withdraw your money. Sound nice? After 30 years, your account will be worth $17,449.40. Not bad, but let me make it better.

Let's say you did the same as above (Initial deposit of $1000, earning 10% per year, and compounded annually), but you also made a monthly contribution of $100 per month. In 30 years, your account would be worth $223,733.73! Now we're talking!

Let's make that better. Let's say that you can afford to save an extra $500 per month, keeping everything else the same as above. How much do you think you'll have? Take a wild guess.

You'd have $1,048,871.06.

""What? Now you're talking my language."

See what I mean? That's the power of compound interest. Of course, not every bank offers this. For this, you'll need to speak to your bank and search online for online accounts that offer you compound interest. Once you do sign up for one, be sure to stick to the plan. Over time, you'll see your money grow significantly.

Now that's an interesting way of making money, isn't it? Do you know what else you can do to really push your finances higher? Investing your money.

INTRODUCTION TO INVESTING

As a teen, you probably think investment is for adults. In a way, you're right, but did you know that you can have your parents or another family member assist you in investing your money into a variety of options that, in return, help you generate profits and more?

Investing your money is the best way to make more money. While compound interest is a great way to make extra money, investing your money can provide you with significantly higher returns.

To give you an idea, Warren Buffett, a billionaire, once bought shares of Berkshire Hathaway at $8 per share (Smith, 2019). He bought such a significant number of shares that he ended up owning most of the company. He did this back in the mid-1960s. He still holds those shares today and each one of those shares can now sell for over $550,000 (Smith, 2019). Needless to say, his shares within this company are in the billions of dollars.

That's the power of clever investments. That is the power of holding your investments and ensuring you see things grow. If you invest wisely, you can earn exponentially higher returns than any savings account. This leads us to the question, what kind of investment options are available for you?

To get started, you'll probably need a custodial account before you can start investing. This type of account is controlled by an adult. Investments are made on behalf of the minor until they turn 18 or 21, depending on the state laws.

If you're younger than the minimum age, you'll need your parent or grandparent to assist you in setting up a custodial account. You can also invest with people that you know, like, and trust! Investing can be done on many levels, so again, ask questions to people you know who are successful investors. Ask them "If you were me, how would you invest my money? Why?" Would you be open to discussing this further so I can learn more?"

The Risk of Investing

No investment is free from risk. Therefore, the very first thing you need is to understand what can go right, what can go wrong, and the likelihood of each. You should also understand your risk profile, which can change at different stages of your life. Your risk profile is how much risk you feel comfortable with at any given time. Some people are more conservative, while others are willing to take on more risk. It's a spectrum, so understanding what type of investor you are is important before investing your money.

Any investment can lead to a potential loss. This is why you should never use borrowed money to invest, whether borrowed from a family member, friend, bank, or credit card. Only use money that you have and that you can afford to lose.

For example, if you only have $1,000, don't invest all of it. Instead, invest $100 periodically. You should also aim at investing money across multiple options. This is called diversification and helps reduce the risk of losses and increase profitability greatly. With that said, this is a more conservative investment viewpoint of someone who doesn't want to take on a lot of risk. Generally, the higher the risk, the bigger the reward.

Let's look at the options you have to help you get started right away.

Stocks

Arguably the most popular investment option of them all, but popular doesn't mean it's the best way to invest. When you buy stocks, you're essentially buying a very small share of the ownership or equity of that particular company. The more stocks you buy, the higher your ownership within the company.

You can make money through stocks in two ways.

- Collect dividends. Some companies offer quarterly payments to their shareholders. These are called dividends.
- Sell your shares at a higher price. Stocks change value all the time. If you buy something at $10 and the price goes higher, say $15, you can sell it off to recover the initial investment as well as the profit.

The change in the prices is called volatility. A higher volatility may fetch you great returns, but a high volatility is also risky.

Therefore, always take into account the volatility of a stock or asset.

I'm not a huge fan of the stock market because I have very little control over the outcome. The stock could increase or go to zero in one day, all without me doing anything to influence the outcome. Another thing I'm not a fan of is the fact that you need to sell to really make a profit, otherwise, it's just a profit on paper. That "paper profit" isn't money in your pocket that you can spend. Lastly, when you're buying and selling stocks you have to be aware that you'll need to pay taxes—if you profit. Other types of investing are more friendly in the areas previously mentioned.

Real Estate

There's no reason why you shouldn't invest in real estate. Every millionaire and billionaire does, and continues to invest in real estate, and for a very good reason. While stocks offer returns, they are a bit of a hit-or-miss. Real estate, on the other hand, ensures you continue to get a monthly income, if rented out properly.

Properties, unlike stocks, are physical assets. Ask any investor and they'll tell you that physical and tangible assets are significantly more rewarding in the long run. Besides, having a property offers you far greater control over your investment than stocks. You get to choose how it looks, when to maintain it, and when to live in it or lease it out.

On top of that, you get huge tax benefits. You can claim depreciation and that can greatly reduce your tax liabilities. That, in simpler terms, is more money in your pocket. There are multiple ways you can use real estate to make money. Some popular options include:

1. Leasing/renting out
2. Airbnb/Vrbo
3. Booking.com
4. Buy, Renovate, Rehabilitate, Refinance (BRRR) model
5. Property flipping

There are some issues with investing in real estate worth noting. Properties aren't liquid assets. While you can sell your properties, it takes a lot of time. It can range anywhere from weeks to months. This means that if you want some quick return, selling a property won't be on the cards.

Then, there's the maintenance. Whether you're living in or renting it out, you'll need to put up with the maintenance cost. You'll need to ensure that the property is always in a livable condition and that it's not damaged. This ensures that the property remains valuable.

Whether you're aiming to buy your property now or later, it's important to take into account all the pros and cons before making a move. You don't want to invest in a property and find out you can't sell it off that easily later on.

Other Types of Investments

Besides the above, you can also invest in the following:

- Certificates of Deposit (CDs): These offer a fixed interest rate for a specific duration. These have higher returns than bonds, but this does mean that you won't be able to access your money until the term is completed.
- Cryptocurrencies: You can choose to buy and hold a variety of cryptocurrencies. However, it's worth noting that cryptocurrency is arguably the riskiest asset to invest in due to its extremely high and unpredictable volatility.

This type of investment is higher risk, and that means it also comes with a higher reward.

How to Get Started With Investing

Getting started while you're still a teenager is perhaps the best way to go about investing. This is because you have plenty of time and significantly more earning potential in the long run. However, don't just jump in, create an account, and start investing. There are a few things you need to do before you get started on that journey.

Gain A Basic Understanding

Information is key. Before investing in anything, you have to familiarize yourself with the basics of investing. Learn how to determine risks, profitability, and loss, and learn all the terms used within the investment world so that you're not caught by surprise.

There are many free resources you can use to do this, depending on which niche you're interested in investing in. Again, I'd talk to people in your family and community and ask them for advice. Remember, advice is just that, you decide in the end, but closely consider their advice.

Learn and Identify Opportunities

Not every day is an opportunity to invest. Somedays, you just need to take a backseat and observe. Somedays, you just know you have to get in.

As a teenager, not every avenue is worth entering. Some are just beyond your reach at the moment as you're probably under 18. However, if you do have an adult involved, you can access virtually all options.

Observe these closely and understand how things work. The more you observe, the more you learn.

Learn More About Investments

Whichever niche you decide to invest in, learn everything you can about it, surround yourself with people in those communities, and ask questions! Just because you own an iPhone and think you know Apple does not mean you should invest in it blindly. Always take time to dig up more information.

Find out if a company has other ventures you aren't familiar with. These will help give you a clearer idea of what a company is involved in, where they may be making money from, and so on.

If you want to learn more about real estate investing, there are clubs, groups, and communities that you can join for free to learn. Maybe it's what you're looking for and you decide to learn more about it. Maybe it's not for you and you learn that as well. Understanding what you don't want to invest in can be just as important as finding the niche that excites you.

All types of investing come with data and research. It's usually a lot of numbers, spreadsheets, calculations, and formulas. When investing, keep in mind WHO you're investing with. Who you trust with your money is just as important as the investment vehicle itself.

Avoid Scams

Many people, social media handles, and websites will claim that they can double or even triple your profits in a ridiculously short time. Please, be aware and be careful of these scams. These investment scams lure people in, make them invest in their so-called schemes, and then disappear with the money.

You can tell something is a potential scam if:

- It sounds too good to be true.
- It offers unusually high and guaranteed results.
- The company is nowhere to be found on the internet or is not well-known.
- The other party insists and pressures you to invest immediately.
- The investment sounds far too complicated to make sense of.

Always run your investment idea by others you trust, as a safeguard against being potentially scammed. Keep this in mind and you should be good to go!

EXERCISE TIME - TEENS & PARENTS

For this chapter, you'll fill out an investment planning worksheet. This will help make financially feasible decisions and will prove to be vital. This exercise is for both parents and teens, and this will likely turn into a conversation as it brings up a lot of great questions that parents and teens should be discussing.

Investment Planning Worksheet

To create an investment planning worksheet, follow the steps below:

1. What goals do you have for your money? Short Term? Long Term? **WRITE IT DOWN!**
2. When do you plan to start investing? **WRITE IT DOWN!**
3. How much risk do you want to take with your money? **WRITE IT DOWN!**
4. When do you need your money back? **WRITE IT DOWN!**
5. Where do you want to invest your money? Real estate? Stock market? Crypto? Lending? **WRITE IT DOWN!**
6. Do you want to invest passively, actively, or both? **WRITE IT DOWN!**

Follow these steps and you can plan the best and most viable options for your next investment move. Remember to WRITE IT DOWN! Update this as often as you need to because your needs and life circumstances will change.

Two Bonus Exercises

Bonus exercise #1 - Here's a quick exercise to help you calculate compound interest. Search for "compound interest calculator" on Google and choose anyone. You'll start with $500 monthly savings that are deposited into this account for the next 10 years.

Calculate how much the account will be worth after 10 years.

Once done, add a zero to your contributions. Instead of $500, make it a $5,000 per month contribution for the same time. Now calculate where your amount will stand.

The lesson here is simple: Think bigger with your numbers and your success will match it.

Bonus exercise #2: If I gave you one penny today, and you were able to double that amount every day for the next 30 days, how much money would you have at the end of day 30?

Take a guess in your head or write it down on a piece of paper, then use a calculator to figure out the exact amount. Ask your friends and family members what they think that number would be and make a game out of it. See who comes closest to the correct answer.

CHAPTER 8
MAPPING YOUR FUTURE

 I will tell you how to become rich. Close the doors. Be fearful when others are greedy. Be greedy when others are fearful.

WARREN BUFFETT

You've come a long way already. However, none of this knowledge will help if you don't know how to use it properly. This chapter will help you get started on the right track. Not only that, but you'll also have a weekly planner that will help you set the right targets, achieve goals, and get in your stride.

CRAFTING YOUR FINANCIAL FREEDOM MAP

This is where you need to take into account everything you've learned. Use all the knowledge to identify your future goals, what they look like, and where you see yourself in the next 10, 20, or even 40 years.

Start noting these down. Everything starts with planning so get in the habit of taking note of everything that's meaningful and important to you.

Whether you intend to become an entrepreneur, an investor, a high-salaried professional, or a little bit of each, you need to start planning how you aim to achieve that.

Use SMART goals. Break the bigger goals down into smaller goals or milestones. With each milestone you achieve, move on to the next one, and the next, until you've achieved the eventual goal. Once you're done, set yourself another goal.

Throughout your life journey, keep on learning—from books, videos, communities, and my favorite, learn from people who have been there before. Keep up-to-date with what's happening so that you can make timely decisions.

Create your budget and stick to it. Use them to generate savings. The more you save, the more you can invest, and put into compound interest accounts, et cetera.

Take your time to understand everything you've learned here. Once ready, start by taking my 30-Day Challenge.

The 5 Week Challenge

This is more of a checklist challenge designed to help you build further financial independence. Repeat this again and again to help you keep the momentum moving forward. You can also modify this plan later, especially when you make more money or have significant life changes.

Week 1

The first week is all about understanding your finances. In this week, you'll need to achieve the following milestones:

1. Track your daily expenses, all of them
2. Create a list of your monthly income. This should include every source including any allowances, grants, dividends, profits, or commissions you get
3. Identify all your fixed and variable expenses
4. Calculate your total monthly expenses
5. Determine your monthly savings rate

This week is aimed at helping you come to terms with your current financial situation. Don't worry if the numbers aren't looking that bright. That can change with time and some effective strategies.

Week 2

The second week is all about setting your financial goals, and this is where most people tend to get things wrong. To start with, no goal is wrong. Every goal is achievable. However, people tend to mix up their goals and make it more complicated than it should be. For example, saving $1000 should technically be a short-term goal. If you write this down as a long-term goal, it's neither worth fighting for nor exciting enough. As a result, you lose your tempo and determination over time and stop pursuing that particular goal.

Therefore, the things you need to do this week include:

1. Setting a short-term goal (such as saving for a new gadget)
2. Setting a medium-term goal (saving for a car perhaps)
3. Setting a long-term goal (saving for college, retirement, a house, et cetera)
4. Prioritize your goals
5. Find out how much you need to save every month to meet these goals in the timeframe you've given yourself

This can be a bit tricky but remember, be realistic.

Week 3

The third week is all about carving out a budget that works for you. Therefore, the things you need to do this week include:

1. Creating a monthly budget based on your current income (all sources)
2. Allocating funds to both fixed and variable expenses
3. Allocating funds for your short, mid, and long-term goals
4. Reviewing your budget to make any adjustments, if and when needed
5. Sticking to your budget

Week 4

The fourth week is all about building and then maintaining good financial habits. These will stick with you for the rest of your life and help you save more, invest more, and eventually reap significantly more as a result.

1. Open a savings account
2. Set up automated transfers
3. Learn more about all investment options available to teenagers
4. Find out the best financial app or tool that you can download and use
5. Learn more about responsible credit use

Week 5

Finally, this week is all about taking action and doing the following:

1. Start using your budget and track your expenses
2. Review your budget every week from here on out and make adjustments where needed
3. Save any additional income, such as tips, commissions, or earnings from side hustles
4. Set up an emergency fund

Additional Tips

- Be sure to attend some personal finance webinars or workshops.
- Discuss your financial goals with your family member or friend, someone you trust.
- Try to find an advisor or a mentor who can help you by offering valuable advice.
- Celebrate the little victories!

Stay Motivated

The start of any journey, let alone one that leads to financial freedom, is exciting. However, as with all things, the journey can quickly cause you to lose motivation. If you take the motivation out, you end up with a journey that starts feeling more like a burden and a responsibility. When that happens, you start pulling away from the entire idea. This is why you need to find ways to keep yourself motivated. To help you, here are some clever ways you can do just that:

- Find your "why." This is what makes you jump out of bed every morning. Write down your why and review it daily by putting it in a place where you're forced to see it every day.
- Set deadlines. The "T" in SMART is timely! Set a realistic timeline to achieve your goal. Remember, don't push your timeline out just to achieve a goal, that's a form of procrastinating.
- Create a positive environment. Put up quotes on your wall, pictures of things that make you happy, read informative and interesting books, and make some like-minded friends that help you stay motivated.
- Embrace challenges. Don't fear them. Embrace them and learn from them.
- Reward yourself. Every now and then, reward yourself for a job well done.
- Track your progress. Instead of looking at how far you still have to go, look back and appreciate how far you've come.
- Visualize a day when you've achieved all your financial goals and are financially independent. Visualize where you are, what you're doing, what you're driving, and dwell in that feeling for 10-15 minutes every day.

- Cut out negativity. If you have people who demotivate you, insult you, or make fun of your dreams, ask yourself if it's worth it to keep those types of relationships in your life. Will those relationships help or hurt your chances of achieving your goals?
- Stay inspired. Whoever inspires you, be sure to follow them. Learn more about them, get to know them, and ask them questions.
- Keep learning throughout your life. Education is infinite if you choose!
- Break down larger goals into smaller goals, to allow for progress, momentum, and consistency.
- Cross off the goals or milestones you've achieved and check back every month to see how much you've achieved.
- Stay organized.
- Find a community with like-minded people who have similar goals and encourage your success.

Common Obstacles

Of course, this journey isn't free from hiccups and obstacles. Some of the most common obstacles you'll face include:

- Lack of financial literacy
- Repaying debts, such as student loans
- Not investing early
- Not taking risks
- Being unable to shake off pressure from peers and family members
- Not understanding goals clearly
- Having second thoughts
- Fear of failure
- Fear of missing out

- Not earning enough money

These challenges are real but not hard to overcome, especially now that you're armed with all the material in this book. As long as you have clarity in life, you'll always be able to achieve your goals.

The journey isn't easy, but it will be worth it! The choices you make from here on out are yours to make. Until you become 18, you'll likely need others to legally help you along this journey. After 18, you'll still need other people's guidance, which I encourage you to take, and take often.

Financial freedom isn't just a dream; it's a reality that many can achieve, including you. It takes a special commitment, knowledge, and willingness. I've given you the foundation and knowledge in this book. Now it's time to start, make a plan, and never give up!

EXERCISE TIME - TEENS & PARENTS

Get started today! Both parents and teens can work on every facet of this book together. Not only will you both learn more about finances and money, but you'll have great conversations that you may never have had before, which opens up a lot of doors for all involved.

CONCLUSION

If only our schools had taught us any of this, we'd all be in a better position to be financially free. Unfortunately, financial literacy is something you must learn on your own. While the schools, colleges, and universities teach you some basic terminology and how the economy works, it's up to you to learn how to become financially free and why you want this for yourself in the first place.

We've grown up believing there's one path in life: Go to college, get a high-paying job, and all will be right in the world. While formal education is important, a job might be good for some, but not for others. Depending on your goals in life, it's up to you to choose what's best for you.

 Formal education will make you a living; self-education will make you a fortune.

JIM ROHN

Money skills are important. Whatever you do in life, wherever you may be, you need to understand how money and finances work, and how to optimize them.

Most teenagers are more interested in spending money as it comes in, without thinking of what a little planning and goal setting can do for their future financial outlook. The goal of this book has been to educate as many teens as possible, give you the tools for financial success, and show you that it's not only possible, but with a little work, education, and drive, you can succeed beyond your wildest dreams. Tackle the challenges now, save, invest, and grow at a young age. You'll struggle and it will be challenging, but the reward will last you a lifetime, and the journey can be its own reward.

You can have any kind of life you want by the time you decide to retire, and you'll do so confidently because you'll know you'll never run out of money. Now that's the kind of financial freedom we all want.

Starting this journey while you're still a teenager is arguably the best step you can take right now. Most people who gain financial literacy in their 30's or 40's regret not learning any of this sooner, including myself! I don't like the word retirement, because one definition I've heard is to take out of service. I always want to be in service and a value to my community. Being financially free at any age allows you to live a great life, as defined by you, while still being in service if you choose to be.

This book may serve as your starting point, but this isn't the only book you need. This is why it's important that you continue your learning journey through experiences and reading more books, blogs, and articles. Be sure to participate in seminars, workshops, and webinars to learn from the industry-leading figures.

I like to listen to my audience and ask for direct feedback. There are a lot of topics that I could have written about but didn't include in this book. **What topics would you like me to include in my next book? More about mindset? More specifics on a certain topic related to investing?**

Please send me a message on Instagram @greg_junge and let me know which topics you want to read about in future books.

With that said, it's time for me to say goodbye to you. I wish you nothing but the best in life. I hope that you found this book helpful, insightful, and above all, informative. Until next time, good luck!

CAN I ASK YOU FOR A FAVOR?

Writing this book has been a challenging yet immensely rewarding journey for me. My goal in writing this book is to share knowledge, educate, and inspire the younger generations and their parents.

Now that you are well-equipped to take control of your finances, I have a favor to ask.

If you haven't already left a review on Amazon, I'd greatly appreciate it if you could. Reviews are crucial for helping others discover and learn from this book, which is my ultimate goal.

Think of your review like the compound interest we discussed earlier. One review from you today adds to the previous reviews, creating powerful momentum. Thank you for your support!

SCAN BELOW TO
LEAVE A REVIEW

Other Recommended Resources to Continue Your Education:

1 Life Roadmap Journal: Student Edition by Tim Rhode

This interactive journal contains activities that go well beyond finances and is a great continuation after reading Teen Money Mindset. It covers Vision Planning, Finances, Relationships, Wellness and much more to elevate yourself to a Life Fully Lived.

Scan QR code for 1 Life Roadmap Journal:

Join DinnerTable, an online teaching platform that helps families (teens and parents) to create value within the home by teaching a strong family dynamic focusing on relationships, finances, responsibility, proactivity, contribution, and much more.

Scan the QR code if you'd like more information to see if this would be a good fit for you and your family.

Scan QR code for DinnerTable:

Personal finance doesn't have to be complicated. In Aaron Nannini's book, Cash Uncomplicated, you'll learn how you can make money simple and create life-changing, generational wealth.

Scan QR code for Cash Uncomplicated:

GLOSSARY

APR: Annual Percentage Return

APY: Annual Percentage Yield

Bear market: When market prices are declining

Blue-chip stocks: Stocks that have substantial value and are from established companies that are known to be leading the industry

Bullish market: When the prices are increasing

Compounding Interest: Interest earned on top of interest

Credit: Having the ability to purchase or buy something now and pay later

Investment: Using money to buy something that is likely to gain value over time and reap profits

Loan: Any amount of money borrowed that must be repaid

ROI: Return on investment (shown in percentage)

Routing number: Nine-digit number, usually found at the bottom of your check, which serves as an identifier

Term: Duration of loan or contract

Wire transfer: Electronic funds transfer (domestic or international)

REFERENCES

Beattie, A. (2022, September 17). *The History Of Money: From Barter To Banknotes.* Investopedia. https://www.investopedia.com/articles/07/roots_of_money.asp

Cardone, G. (2015, March 2). *Don't Fall for These 12 Mental Money Traps.* Entrepreneur. https://www.entrepreneur.com/money-finance/dont-fall-for-these-12-mental-money-traps/242865

CNB. (n.d.). *What Is True About Emotions and Financial Decisions?* City National Bank. https://www.cnb.com/personal-banking/insights/emotions-and-financial-decisions.html

CoinGecko. (n.d.). *Cryptocurrency Prices, Charts, and Crypto Market Cap.* https://www.coingecko.com/

Daly, L. (2022, February 25). *How Many Cryptocurrencies Are There?* The Motley Fool. https://www.fool.com/investing/stock-market/market-sectors/financials/cryptocurrency-stocks/how-many-cryptocurrencies-are-there/

Gowtham, S. (2023, July 31). *Financial System: What is it, Components, Functions & Challenges.* Happay. https://happay.com/blog/financial-system/

Johnson, P. (2021, May 25). *Financial System - Meaning, Components, Functions.* WallStreetMojo. https://www.wallstreetmojo.com/financial-system/

Knueven, L. (2024, January 4). *The average savings account interest rate.* Business Insider. https://www.businessinsider.com/personal-finance/average-savings-account-interest-rate

Lake, R. (2022, July 5). *Budgeting for teens: What you need to know.* The Balance. https://www.thebalancemoney.com/how-to-teach-your-teen-about-budgeting-4160105

Rivera, D. (2023, July 26). *16 Impulse Buying Statistics Retailers Should Know in 2023.* Fit Small Business. https://fitsmallbusiness.com/impulse-buying-statistics/

Schmohe, A. (2021, March 10). *From David to Goliath: 8 Brands that Started as Hobbies.* The Vector Impact by Vector Marketing. https://www.thevectorimpact.com/brands-that-started-as-hobbies/

Schulz, M. (2024, January 16). *2021 Credit Card Debt Statistics.* LendingTree. https://www.lendingtree.com/credit-cards/credit-card-debt-statistics/

Smith, L. (2019). *Warren Buffett: The Road To Riches.* Investopedia. https://www.investopedia.com/articles/financial-theory/08/buffetts-road-to-riches.asp

Teen Money Mindset Workbook for Teens and Adults

Attention Parents

Ready to equip your teens with essential financial skills? This workbook is designed for everyone—work through it together, spark discussions, and ask the important questions!

Future Money Masters - Teens

Ready to level up your financial game? This workbook is all about helping you build key money skills, and you can even work through it with your parents if you'd like. Start the conversation and take action!

CHAPTER 1:
Exercises: The Language of Money and the Crypto Craze

Teen Question:
What are some financial terms you've heard but don't fully understand? Pick one and explain what it means in your own words. Then, ask an adult to help further explain it and start a conversation.

_____

_____

_____

Adult Question:
How has your understanding of financial concepts changed over time? What financial terms or concepts do you wish you had learned earlier?

_____

_____

_____

Teen Journaling Prompt:
Write about your first experience with money. How did it feel, and what did you learn from it?

_____

_____

_____

Adult Journaling Prompt:
Write about your first experience with money. How did it feel, and what did you learn from it?

_____

_____

_____

CHAPTER 2:
Exercises: Money Mindset Magic

Teen Question:

How do you feel when you think about money? Do you see it as something positive, negative, or neutral? Why?

_____

_____

_____

Adult Question:

How do you talk about money with the teens in your life, like your children, nieces, or nephews? Are you positively presenting money, or does it come across negatively?

_____

_____

_____

Teen Journaling Prompt:

Write about a time when you felt confident about money and a time when you felt unsure. What was different in each situation, and how can you develop a positive money mindset?

_____

_____

_____

Adult Journaling Prompt:

Reflect on how your mindset about money has evolved. What limiting beliefs about money have you overcome, and which ones are still holding you back?

_____

_____

_____

CHAPTER 3:
Exercises: Credit Crush

Teen Question:
What do you think credit is, and why do you think it's important? What are some ways you can start building good credit today?

_____

_____

_____

Adult Question:
What was your experience when you first got access to credit? How has managing credit helped or hindered your financial goals?

_____

_____

_____

Teen Journaling Prompt:
Imagine you're about to get your first credit card. Write about how you would use it responsibly and what you can do to avoid carrying debt.

_____

_____

_____

Adult Journaling Prompt:
Reflect on your current credit habits. What strategies have you used to maintain good credit, and what could you improve to avoid or manage debt better?

_____

_____

_____

CHAPTER 4:
Exercises: Crafting Your Budget Masterpiece

Teen Question:

What are the most important things you would include in your personal budget?

_____

_____

_____

Adult Question:

What budgeting method has worked best for you in the past, and why? If you don't budget, what has stopped you from creating one?

_____

_____

_____

Teen Journaling Prompt:

After creating your budger from the exercise in chapter 4, reflect on how you felt about the process. Did you enjoy it? Are you looking at it on a daily or weekly basis?

_____

_____

_____

Adult Journaling Prompt:

Think about a time when sticking to a budget helped you reach a financial goal. What strategies did you use, and how can you apply those strategies in the future? How can you teach others in your life these strategies?

_____

_____

_____

CHAPTER 5:
The Saving Adventure Awaits

Teen Question:

What are three things you want to save for, and why? Where is the money coming from to build up your savings account?

_____

_____

_____

Adult Question:

What savings goal are you currently working toward, and how did you decide on that goal? What challenges have you faced in staying consistent with saving?

_____

_____

_____

Teen Journaling Prompt:

Write about your biggest savings goal. How long will it take to reach it, and what steps can you take each week or month to stay on track?

_____

_____

_____

Adult Journaling Prompt:

Reflect on your relationship with saving. Do you find it easy or difficult to set money aside? What emotional or mental barriers do you face in prioritizing savings?

_____

_____

_____

CHAPTER 6:
Turning Your Passions into Profit

Teen Question:

Do you have any hobbies or passions that you are thinking of turning into a side hustle or business? If so, write down the ones that immediately come to mind.

_____

_____

_____

Adult Question:

Have you ever tried to monetize a passion? What were the challenges, and what advice would you give to someone starting out?

_____

_____

_____

Teen Journaling Prompt:

Pick a hobby or passion from above and brainstorm ways you could earn money from it. What resources or tools would you need? How would you advertise your business?

_____

_____

_____

Adult Journaling Prompt:

If you have tried to monetize a hobby or profit, how did it go? What went right and what went wrong? If you haven't, is there one or two hobbies that you are considering?

_____

_____

_____

CHAPTER 7:
Turning Your Passions into Profit

Teen Question:
What does investing mean to you? Why do you think it's important to start learning about it now?

_____

_____

_____

Adult Question:
How did you first get introduced to investing, and what do you wish you had known before starting? What advice would you give to someone just starting?

_____

_____

_____

Teen Journaling Prompt:
Write about your understanding of investing in real estate or another form of investing. What excites or scares you about it, and what do you want to learn more about?

_____

_____

_____

Adult Journaling Prompt:
Reflect on your investment journey. What's been your biggest win and your biggest lesson? How do you plan to refine your investment strategy going forward?

_____

_____

_____

CHAPTER 8:
Mapping Your Future

Teen Question:

What does financial freedom mean to you? How are you going to implement everything you've learned in this book and put it into practice in real life?

_____

_____

_____

Adult Question:

What does your financial freedom map look like? How has your definition of financial independence changed as you've gotten older?

_____

_____

_____

Teen Journaling Prompt:

Create a vision board or write a detailed plan of where you see yourself financially in 5, 10, and 20 years. What are the milestones along the way?

_____

_____

_____

Adult Journaling Prompt:

Reflect on your financial goals. Where do you see yourself in the next 10 years? What habits or actions do you need to adopt to make that vision a reality?

_____

_____

_____

(Optional addition for parents to fill out with teens)

Exercise 1: Joint Goal Setting

Parents and teens: Write down one shared financial goal you want to achieve together.

Our goal is:

_____

_____

_____

Steps we will take:

1. _____

2. _____

3. _____

Exercise 2: Accountability Partner

Create a weekly or monthly check-in system where teens and parents can review progress toward financial goals.

Our check-in dates will be:

_____   _____

_____   _____

_____   _____